PREACHING
IN THE
CONTEXT
OF
WORSHIP

PREACHING
IN THE
CONTEXT
OF
WORSHIP

David M. Greenhaw
and Ronald J. Allen
EDITORS

Chalice Press®

St. Louis, Missouri

Bible quotations, unless otherwise noted, are from the *New Revised Standard Version Bible,* copyright 1989, Division of Christian Education of the National Council of the Churches of Christ in the United States of America. Used by permission. All rights reserved.

Cover design and art direction: Michael Domínguez
Cover photo: © Copyright 1998 Michael Domínguez
Interior design: Elizabeth Wright

This book is printed on acid-free, recycled paper.

Visit Chalice Press on the World Wide Web at
www.chalicepress.com

10 9 8 7 6 5 4 3 2 1   00 01 02 03 04

Library of Congress Cataloging–in–Publication Data

Preaching in the context of worship / edited by David M. Greenhaw and Ronald J. Allen.
    p. cm.
    Includes bibliographical references and index.
    ISBN 0-8272-2956-9
    1. Preaching. 2. Public worship. I. Greenhaw, David M. II. Allen, Ronald J. (Ronald James)
BV4211.2 .P736 2000
251–dc21   99-050555

Printed in the United States of America

Contents

Contributors

Marian Young Adell (Ph.D., Drew University) is pastor of Community United Methodist Church in Dayton, Ohio.

Ronald J. Allen (Ph.D., Drew University) is Nettie Sweeney and Hugh Th. Miller Professor of Preaching and New Testament at Christian Theological Seminary, Indianapolis, Indiana.

Shelley E. Cochran (Ph.D., Drew University) is a Presbyterian minister living in Rochester, New York. She is the author of *The Pastor's Underground Guide to the Revised Common Lectionary* (3 volumes).

Heather Murray Elkins (Ph.D., Drew University) is Academic Associate Dean and Associate Professor of Worship and Liturgical Studies at the Theological School, Drew University, Madison, New Jersey.

David M. Greenhaw (Ph.D., Drew University) is President of Eden Theological Seminary, St. Louis, Missouri.

Douglas Gwyn (Ph.D., Drew University) is Scholar in Residence at Pendle Hill, Wallingford, Pennsylvania.

Robin L. Meyers (Ph.D., University of Oklahoma; D.Min., Drew University) is pastor of Mayflower Congregational Church, United Church of Christ, and director of the M.A. program at Oklahoma City University, both in Oklahoma City, Oklahoma.

Koo Yong Na (Ph.D., Drew University) is pastor of Korean Community Church of New Jersey–United Methodist in Leonia, New Jersey.

Rochelle A. Stackhouse (Ph.D., Drew University) is associate pastor of Glen Ridge Congregational Church, Hackensack, New Jersey, and adjunct professor at Hartford Seminary, Hartford, Connecticut.

Paul Scott Wilson (Ph.D., University of London) is Professor of Preaching and Worship at Emmanuel College, University of Toronto, Toronto, Ontario, Canada.

Preface

This book serves two purposes. First, it explores key issues with respect to preaching in the context of worship. We hope that this collection of ten essays by ten authors will be of interest to pastors who preach weekly in services of worship and to seminary classes in both preaching and worship. Although each chapter is by a different author, the various chapters are designed to work together toward a comprehensive exploration of preaching in the worship setting. Second, the collection honors Charles L. Rice, professor of homiletics in the theological and graduate schools, Drew University, for whom the relationship between preaching and worship has been a central focus for more than thirty years.

For excellent administrative support, we want to thank Denise Killebrew, assistant to the president of Eden Theological Seminary, and Joyce Krauser, secretary to the faculty at Christian Theological Seminary. These two administrators regard their daily work as ministries in behalf of the gospel. They provided excellent technical guidance, and they helped us manage the development of this project in concert with our wider lives. They offered considered editorial wisdom. We also thank E. Byron Anderson, assistant professor of worship and director of the chapel at Christian Theological Seminary, for helping us with the basic concepts, directions, and themes of this book.

Introduction

Worship is at the center of the Christian life. Worship is both expressive and formative. In liturgy the church expresses its thoughts and feelings to God through hymns, prayers, and other words. The sermon, too, is sometimes a means through which the Christian community expresses itself to God. God is the focus of Christian worship. We honor and praise God. We talk with God. We give ourselves to God. We receive gifts from God. Worship is also formative. The language and actions of worship form the ways in which we understand God, Christ, the Holy Spirit, the church, and the world. The service of worship forms Christian faith and community less by transmitting information about God and more by helping us name the Divine and the world through the words and actions of the liturgy. When we sing, "Jesus, thou art all compassion, pure unbounded love, thou art,"[1] we learn that Jesus is, indeed, pure, unbounded love.

Indeed, the service of worship and its constituent parts represent the relationship of God and the human community. And in worship Christians represent our relationship with one another and with the world. For instance, when we serve the loaf and the cup to one another, we symbolize (represent) that the Christian community is one defined by mutual service.[2]

Christian preaching takes place in two arenas. (1) Most preaching takes place in services of worship. These services include the weekly worship of the church as well as particular occasions beyond weekly worship, such as the wedding and the funeral. Such services and sermons typically presume established communities of believers. (2) Preaching can also be for the purpose of evangelism, that is, offering the gospel to people who have not accepted the gospel as the basis for their self-understanding and actions. Evangelistic preaching sometimes takes place outside the religious community. The essays in this volume are oriented toward the first arena.

Preaching is a prominent part of most services of worship in the church. The setting in which the sermon takes place is liturgical.

---

[1]Charles Wesley, "Love Divine, All Loves Excelling," in *Chalice Hymnal* (St. Louis: Chalice Press, 1995), no. 517.

[2]For further discussion of these aspects of worship, see Clark M. Williamson and Ronald J. Allen, *Adventures of the Spirit: A Guide to Worship from the Perspective of Process Theology* (Lanham, Md.: University Press of America, 1997), 61–88.

Despite this prominence and setting, the relationship between the sermon and its context in worship has received relatively little attention from pastors and from scholars in the fields of preaching and worship. Preaching textbooks typically devote only a chapter or a part of a chapter to this subject. Parish ministers and scholars write occasional articles with this focus. But few in the church turn their full and sustained gaze on this topic.

The subject of preaching in the liturgical setting deserves consideration in its own right as a part of the church's normative reflection on worship and preaching. In addition, the time is ripe for such a consideration. Liturgical renewal is taking place in many congregations and denominations in the Christian community. This renewal ranges from the fresh appropriation of classical motifs in worship, sparked by the Second Vatican Council, that are coming to full bloom in the Roman Catholic Church and in many historic Protestant churches, to contemporary services that make extensive use of soft-rock music and media. The writers in this book largely concentrate on the liturgical renewal movement that began with Vatican II and has spread into many long-established Protestant churches. These churches include the African Methodist Episcopal Church, the African Methodist Episcopal Zion Church, the Christian Church (Disciples of Christ), the Christian Methodist Episcopal Church, the Episcopal Church, the United Methodist Church, the Reformed Church in America, the United Presbyterian Church (USA), and the United Church of Christ. Other churches and movements also show effects of this movement.

Preaching in the Context of Worship honors Charles L. Rice, who, since 1970, has served as professor of homiletics in the theological and graduate schools of Drew University. Father Rice is one of the few pastor-scholars to consider the mutuality of preaching and worship. The publication of his evocative *The Embodied Word* (1991) coincided with the recognition that his own spiritual journey was one of moving ever closer to the loaf and the cup as the center of the experience of the Christian community.[3] Father Rice grew up as a Southern Baptist and was ordained after receiving the M.Div. at Southern Baptist Theological Seminary. He completed the Master of Sacred Theology at Union Theological Seminary, New York, where he began a lifelong friendship with Edmund A. Steimle. He completed the Ph.D. and served as a dean for students at Duke University. As a young adult, he became a member of the United Church of Christ.

[3]Charles L. Rice, *The Embodied Word: Preaching as Art and Liturgy,* Fortress Resources for Preaching (Minneapolis: Fortress Press, 1991).

In his middle years he began to attend a weekday service of the eucharist at an Episcopal church located down the street from Drew and found himself drawn to that rich, multilayered tradition of worship that includes both word and sacrament. He is now set aside as a priest in the Episcopal Church and frequently serves as both a parish priest and as a professor in a theological school.

All but two of the contributors to this volume were Ph.D. students of Professor Rice in the graduate school of Drew University. The Drew graduate program in homiletics calls for a student to major in a classical theological discipline (e.g., Bible, church history, systematic theology) with significant work in homiletics and hermeneutics. Charles Rice served as the homiletics advisor for each of the eight writers who completed the Ph.D. at Drew. Robin L. Meyers completed the D.Min. at Drew while working with Professor Rice. Paul Scott Wilson began his academic life as a scholar of literary criticism. When Professor Wilson was called to teach preaching, he studied with Professor Rice and considers Professor Rice a mentor.

Father Rice himself articulates underlying principles that guide the writers in the present volume. Because the service of worship is (or should be) an integrated whole, the liturgy can help shape the content and tone of the sermon. The sermon can take its cues from its place in the service of worship, the season of the Christian year, the lectionary readings, and the pastoral setting of the congregation. The sermon does not exist as an independent entity within the service, but draws its life from, and contributes to, the liturgy. Not only that, but at its optimum preaching takes place in a context that centers in the breaking of the loaf. Furthermore, Charles Rice is one of the most insistent voices in the homiletics community today calling for preaching to become a work of the community. Preaching should be,

> at every point, in its inception, preparation and delivery—whatever its distinguishing characteristics, and however much it may depend upon the preacher's person and craft—a function of the community of the baptized gathered around the holy table. Even the content of the sermon—its language coming from this very community, is analogous to the sacraments. Like bread, wine, and water, and words and idiom, stories and images of the very time and place become, in the sermon, the gifts of God for the people of God.[4]

---

[4]Ibid., 54.

The sermon is part of the journey of the people to the table.[5]

Indeed, Father Rice would have us preach from the table, a place from which he hopes the preacher can see the baptistery. Such a theological location can help the preacher with the theological tone of the sermon. "This is the place, at the table, where gospel preaching is most assured, and the preacher who stands there with the baptistery in full view will be more inclined to give thanks than to complain, to bless than to curse."[6] Ethical consequences also follow. "Placing preaching firmly in the liturgy is more likely to keep us close to the gospel and away from chauvinism, moralism, parochialism, and the unworthy agendas that crowd in upon us. Keeping preaching close to the sacrament is the best way to prevent its perversion."[7] The connection between preaching and the liturgy, particularly the table, is so vital that Rice counsels,

> Even where there is no Communion, the order of service can be Eucharist, with the offering and prayers appearing at the same places as on Communion Sunday. Simply by standing at the table for the prayers of the people and the Lord's Prayer, the presiding minister can gather the community in such a way as to connect the whole service with the Eucharist. (To effect this visual symbol, it would be important to keep the communion table clear, so that its proper use is always in view.) This will be all the more effective if the pastoral prayer—one more clericalism—gives way to bidding prayers that invite the congregation to do its liturgical work around the table, in a kind of "dry communion."[8]

Not surprisingly, Rice admonishes, "There is, of course, no substitute for breaking bread together."[9]

The contributors to *Preaching in the Context of Worship* join our teacher in thinking that preaching should be understood as an integral part of worship. In different degrees, we join Father Rice in moving toward a liturgically-shaped preaching. The essays in this book seek to explore, augment, and sharpen some of the concerns of

---

[5]One of the contributors, Douglas Gwyn, is a minister in the Society of Friends. The Friends are sometimes described as nonsacramental because they do not practice water baptism or serve the loaf and the cup. While not meaning to oversimplify, we still see a positive contact between the tradition of the Friends and Professor Rice's major point. Friends encounter the divine presence, in part, through silence. The silence has a sacramental dimension in that it mediates the knowledge of God.

[6]Rice, *The Embodied Word,* 55.

[7]Ibid., 56.

[8]Ibid., 62.

[9]Ibid.

Professor Rice as well as to break new ground and to offer occasional alternative points of view. Chapter 1, by Marian Young Adell, frames this exploration by tracing developments in the relationship of preaching and worship in the movement toward the renewal of worship in the last thirty years that has come about in response to the liturgical calls of the Second Vatican Council. In chapter 2, Heather Murray Elkins discusses the connection of identity and community as they are formed in the midst of worship and preaching. In chapter 3, Robin L. Meyers notes ways in which the service of worship amplifies the voice of the preacher and ways in which the sermon echoes the liturgy. Paul Scott Wilson illuminates the vital connection between preaching and the sacrament of holy communion in chapter 4. In chapter 5, Shelley E. Cochran sketches the multifaceted interrelatedness among preaching, worship, the Christian year, and The Revised Common Lectionary. She takes a critical approach to these matters. David M. Greenhaw's subject in chapter 6 is worship, preaching, and change. He discusses the interaction between these topics by focusing on culture as a setting for worship and on art as a mode of culture. In chapter 7, Rochelle A. Stackhouse draws our attention to ways in which music and preaching can work together in worship. Music, in fact, is proclamation no less than the sermon. The sermon that has a certain musicality is a double blessing. Douglas Gwyn, in chapter 8, offers practical guidance whereby a congregation can exercise the priesthood of all believers by entering into the process of preparing the sermon with the preacher. The church that follows Gwyn's proposal will become, as Rice hopes, a preaching community. Ronald J. Allen, in chapter 9, considers preaching in contexts of worship that are found outside the weekly service—especially a funeral, a wedding, an ecumenical service, an interreligious service, and a service in connection with a civic event. Koo Yong Na concludes the book with chapter 10 by reflecting on the tensions that inhere in preaching and worship in racial and ethnic congregations that attempt to maintain a particular cultural identity while making their way through a dominant culture that is quite different.

We are moved to honor Professor Rice not only because he is a groundbreaking scholar, a splendid teacher, an engaging preacher, and a significant mentor, but because he is one of the most sensitive human beings and Christians we have known. Indeed, to be in his presence—the haunting gaze of his eyes, the compassionate feel of his being, the gentle way he is in the world—is to experience something of the reign of God. In language that is important to the topic of this book, Charles is a visible Word.

Bibliography of Major Works of Charles L. Rice

Books

The Embodied Word: Preaching as Art and Liturgy. Fortress Resources for Preaching. Minneapolis: Fortress Press, 1991.

Preaching the Story. With Edmund A. Steimle and Morris J. Niedenthal. Philadelphia: Fortress Press, 1980.

Proclamation: Aids for Interpreting the Lessons of the Church Year. Easter. Series B. With J. Louis Martyn. Philadelphia: Fortress Press, 1975.

Interpretation and Imagination: The Preacher and Contemporary Literature. Philadelphia: Fortress Press, 1970.

Articles, Chapters in Books, and Sermons

"Sermon for Easter Day," in *Patterns for Preaching: A Sermon Sampler.* Edited by Ronald J. Allen. St. Louis: Chalice Press, 1998, 112–16.

"Arts and Preaching," in *Concise Encyclopedia of Preaching.* Edited by William H. Willimon and Richard Lischer. Louisville, Ky.: Westminster John Knox Press, 1995, 16–19.

"From the Sixteenth Floor," in *A Chorus of Witnesses.* Edited by Thomas G. Long and Cornelius Plantinga, Jr. Grand Rapids, Mich.: William B. Eerdmans Publishing Co., 1994, 53–61.

"Preaching about the Ecumenical Church: Beyond the Melting Pot," in *Preaching In and Out of Season.* Edited by Thomas G. Long and Neely D. McCarter. Louisville, Ky.: Westminster/John Knox Press, 1990, 91–103.

"A Response to 'Drew's Theological Ethos: In Quest of Multicultural Theological Education,'" *Drew Gateway* 59 (1989): 54–59.

"Eikon and Eiron: Faith as Imagination," *Saint Luke's Journal of Theology* 32 (1989): 249–56.

"Liturgical Springtime: A Visit to Taizé," *Drew Gateway* 55, no. 1 (1984): 42–48.

"Shaping Sermons by the Interplay of Text and Metaphor," in *Preaching Biblically.* Edited by Don M. Wardlaw. Philadelphia: Westminster Press, 1983, 101–20.

"Just Church Bells: One Man's View of Preaching Today," *Drew Gateway* 49, no. 3 (1979): 31–37. Also published as "Preaching Today: One Man's View," in *Reading, Preaching, and Celebrating the Word.* Edited by J. Paul Marcoux. Palm Springs, Fla.: Sunday Publications, 1980, 19–26.

"The Preacher as Storyteller," *Union Seminary Quarterly Review* 31 (1976): 182–97. Also published in *Drew Gateway* 46, no. 1–3 (1975–76): 11–28.

"Ministry in Community: A Sermon on Acts 2:41–47," *Drew Gateway* 44 (1974): 100–5.

"An Uncommonly Common Grace," in *Preaching in the Witnessing Community.* Edited by Herman G. Stuempfle, Jr. Philadelphia: Fortress Press, 1973, 62–68.

"Chronicle of a Sermon: Word-Event as Theological Integration," *Drew Gateway* 41 (1971): 169–80.

"The Expressive Style in Preaching," *Princeton Seminary Bulletin* 64 (1971): 30–42.

"Assimilation or Cultural Pluralism?" *The Christian Century* 86 (1969): 945–47.

"The First and the Last," *Duke Divinity School Review* 30 (1965): 137–41.

Editor

Word and Witness: A Complete Resource for Celebrating and Proclaiming the Gospel, 1976–1991.

1

PREACHING IN THE RENEWAL
OF WORSHIP IN THE LAST
THIRTY YEARS

Marian Young Adell

Thirty years ago Vatican II shook the church with its radical reforms, undoing and modifying doctrines and worship practices that
had stood for some four hundred years. It stands as a watershed event,
a clear point in history when subsequent events are forever changed
because of a particular occurrence. The changes in worship instituted in the Roman Catholic Church as a result of the Second Vatican
Council (Vatican II) were the consequence of nearly one hundred
years of biblical scholarship and scholarly investigation into the worship of the early church. This scholarship sought to better understand the worship of that time so that the church could recover more
of both the biblical witness and the early church tradition. Also influ-
encing the reforms were numerous liturgical conferences that questioned how the church could be both more faithful to the Christian
witness found in the church's historic tradition and more relevant to
the church today. As for liturgical renewal, the Protestant churches
were in dialogue with both Protestant and Roman Catholic liturgical
scholars.[1] And it was a Protestant church that first instituted many of
the reforms that scholarship and the conferences suggested. It was
the formation of the Church of South India (CSI) in 1947 that first
led to the development of worship that combined strands of Anglican,

---

[1]Massey Hamilton Shepherd, Jr., *The Liturgical Renewal of the Church* (New York:
Oxford University Press, 1960), briefly recounts the major people and events that
shaped the liturgical movement of Protestants and Roman Catholics before Vatican II.

Protestant, and Orthodox traditions with the culture of South India.[2] Many of the innovations of the CSI are found in the newer liturgies of many denominations today.

When looking at worship renewal over the past thirty years, many believe that only the order of the worship service is involved. Previously, many churches modeled their worship after one of two patterns. The first is found in Isaiah 6: praise, confession and pardon, hearing God's word, and departing into the world to do God's bidding. The second follows the order of worship found in the revivals of the nineteenth century: singing, prayer, preaching for decision, and gathering in the harvest of new converts. However, with the worship renewal, Luke 24 becomes the model: hearing the scripture interpreted through a christological lens and then celebrating the eucharist, when Christ is known to the gathered community in the breaking of the bread. For many congregants the most noticeable change is that the "offering" and the "pastoral prayer" or "prayers of the people" follow the sermon. However, the change in the order of the service is just the tip of the iceberg, as the following major characteristics of worship renewal suggest: (1) a recovery of the church as community, (2) participation of all worshipers, (3) a recovery of the early church model, (4) a rediscovery of the Bible, (5) a rediscovery of the eucharist, (6) an emphasis on the vernacular and cultural context, (7) the rediscovery of other Christian traditions, and (8) an emphasis on proclamation and social involvement.[3]

Community

One of the hallmarks of our present age is individualism. We have heard of the "rugged individual" from westerns and current action movies. On our bookshelves are any number of self-help books. This pervasive individualism, many believe, is the logical culmination of the Enlightenment. Worship is not immune to cultural individualism. Worship that reflects this is understood either as the individual communing with God with little if any interaction with other worshipers or as the validity of worship being based on an individual's spiritual uplifting. Liberal religious writings of the first

---

[2]For more information see T. S. Garrett, "An Introduction and Commentary," in *The Liturgy of the Church of South India* (London: Oxford University Press, 1952); idem, *Worship in the Church of South India* (Richmond, Va.: John Knox Press, 1958); and S. M. Gibbard, "Liturgical Life in the Church of South India," *Studia Liturgica* 3 (1964): 193–209.

[3]I am indebted to John Fenwick and Bryan Spinks for these helpful categories from *Worship in Transition* (New York: Continuum, 1995), 5–11.

part of this century focused on the individual's experience of and quest for God.[4] In the more evangelical camp, certain groups have defined Christianity only in terms of the individual "receiving Christ." Campus Crusade, with its four spiritual laws, and televangelism, with its pitch to the individual, often focus only on the individualized message of "me and Jesus." The need for or importance of the church is lost for both classical liberals and conservatives.

One of the hallmarks of worship renewal is the recovery of the New Testament concept of the church as the body of Christ. There is no Christianity without the church. Christ is a bodiless head without the church. This image of the church as the body of Christ encompasses both unity and diversity while maintaining the uniqueness of the individual within the larger context of the community, the church. This image becomes the basis for both the ministry of the laity and the vital importance of that ministry. The days of the pastor of the church being *the* minister of the church are over in the churches touched by this worship renewal. This image recovers the connection and bond that exist between the people present at worship and then beyond the individual congregation to the bonds that exist between the people of the various churches. This image strengthens ecumenical cooperation between churches and communions. To reinforce the sense of community, many worship services now have a time of passing the peace or greeting one another, and many hold hands while praying the Lord's Prayer. The handshake and greeting acknowledge the other worshipers in a physical and concrete way. The prayers of the people may actually be voiced by different members of the congregation. The language in prayers and hymns changes from "me" to "us" and from "I" to "we." This recovery of community and this change in language address the dominant culture with its individualism. The African American and Hispanic churches reflect their cultures' greater sense of community. These groups understand that the individual cannot exist without community. The dominant culture hopefully is beginning to understand this truth.

Participation

In the movie *The Song of Bernadette,* worship involved personal prayers and the rosary while the priest said the mass in the foreign language of Latin. There was no relationship in worship between the

---

[4]For example, in the classics, see Rudolf Otto, *The Idea of the Holy* (London: Oxford University Press, 1936); William James, *The Varieties of Religious Experience* (Cambridge, Mass.: Harvard University Press, 1985); or the theology of Paul Tillich.

layperson and the priest, no congregational participation in this way of worship except viewing the raised host and the raised cup. In many Protestant churches, there was often no congregational participation beyond listening to the sermon, singing some hymns, and passing the offering plate. With the image of the body of Christ, all members of Christ's body are to participate in worship, and the whole person is to participate in worship, not just the ear and the mind. In fact, *leitourgia,* the Greek word for worship, means work. Worship involves the community, not just the preachers or the priests. Moreover, worship involves all the senses: sight, sound, touch, taste, and smell. Worship is no longer a spectacle, but a community action. So now with the liturgical renewal, there is more congregational participation and singing. There are sung/spoken responses in the Lord's supper, there are sung antiphons with the psalms. The newer denominational hymnals have set the hymn tunes within the range of most people to facilitate singing. Perhaps one of the most notable shifts is the participation of children in worship. Few Protestant churches with children do not now have a children's moment. And the movement for the inclusion of children in worship, and not banishing them to "children's church," reflects that, indeed, when baptized, children become part of the body of Christ and are to worship together with adults as part of that body. The movement for greater participation is the impetus for the remodeling of worship spaces and church buildings so that those with wheelchairs may participate and for the provision of signing for the deaf during worship services.

Rediscovery of the Early Church Model

Liturgical scholarship began to focus on the *Apology of Justin Martyr,* written around 155 C.E. in Rome, and *The Apostolic Tradition* of Hippolytus, written around 200 C.E. also in Rome, as models of early church worship.[5] Both of these documents describe baptism and the Lord's Day service, which always ended with the eucharist. *Eucharist* is Greek for "thanksgiving." There were two parts of the service: the service of the Word and the service of the table. The service of the Word was open to everyone and consisted of (1) reading from the prophets and the apostles; (2) the sermon; (3) the community prayer (the unbaptized were led out of the worship service before prayer, since this sacred activity was for the body of Christ); and (4) after prayer, everyone's greeting one another with a kiss, a sign of the

---

[5]Bard Thompson, *Liturgies of the Western Church* (Philadelphia: Fortress Press, 1961), 3–24.

reconciliation. The service of the table consisted of (1) the offering, bringing the bread and a cup of wine mingled with water to the president; (2) the president's offering a prayer of thanksgiving to God for creation by the Word, thanksgiving for incarnation of the Word, and redemption through the passion of the Word, and then reciting the institutional narrative and an *epiclesis* or invocation of the Holy Spirit, with the assembly shouting "Amen" to signify their assent at the end of this prayer; (3) the president's breaking the bread; and (4) the deacons' serving the bread and wine to everyone present.

Biblical scholars discovered that one of the proclamations of the early church was that Jesus Christ was risen. The tenor of the early church services was joyous, celebrating the victorious Christ who overcame sin and death, present with his people. This celebration was in marked contrast to the communion services based on the medieval liturgies, which were more penitential in nature and focused on the suffering and death of Jesus on the cross. Although the reformers of the sixteenth century changed many things, they kept the contrite nature of the Lord's supper with a focus on the cross, and the meaning of the Lord's supper found primarily in the forgiveness of sins.

Most of the "newer" rituals and liturgies that have been developed by various denominations and constituencies are influenced by Justin Martyr and Hippolytus. In a world facing the myriad problems of today, the joy of the Lord that the early church, in the midst of persecution, had in its worship is appealing to us. Another compelling reason for using these services as models is that they were in use before all the divisions in the church: before the Reformation of the sixteenth century, and even before the Roman Catholic and Orthodox schism that became irreparable by the end of the eleventh century. Another recovery from the early church has been the church year. Beginning with Advent, the church year celebrates the life and resurrection of Christ and the founding and development of the church. The story of the incarnation and the resurrection that culminates with Pentecost is relived annually through worship attentive to the Christian seasons.[6]

Rediscovery of the Bible

Although the cry of the sixteenth-century Reformation was *"Sola Scriptura,"* or scripture alone, and the reformers had chapters of

---

[6]Adolf Adam, *The Liturgical Year: Its History and Its Meaning After the Reform of the Liturgy* (New York: Pueblo Publishing, 1981); and Hoyt L. Hickman, et al., *The New Handbook of the Christian Year* (Nashville: Abingdon Press, 1992).

scripture read as part of the service, a more common practice in many Protestant churches until recently was the reading of a single verse of scripture as a jumping-off point for the sermon. Part of the renewal is allowing scripture as the living word of God to form the community in worship, so that in Sunday worship there are four readings: Hebrew Scripture, Psalm, Epistle, and Gospel. Various lectionaries, or prescribed readings for each Sunday, have been developed to provide for an orderly overview of scripture. The one currently in use in North America is The Revised Common Lectionary developed by the Consultation on Common Texts in 1992, revising their 1983 lectionary. There are several assumptions that underlie their choice of scripture: (1) It is for the weekly celebration of the Lord's Day, a festival for the proclamation of the gospel of Jesus Christ. Thus, the gospel reading is primary, and the period from the Reign of Christ (the Sunday before Advent) through Trinity Sunday (the Sunday after Pentecost) dictates the other readings. (2) The lections are chosen to relate to the Christian calendar, from Advent to Epiphany, the celebration of the Incarnation (Christmas), and then from Lent to Pentecost, the celebration of the Resurrection (Easter). (3) Each year of the three-year cycle focuses on one of the synoptic gospels. The gospel of John is used at Christmas and Easter and in year B to supplement Mark.[7] The revision added more lections about women and revised the Hebrew Scripture readings following Pentecost, along with some technical fine-tuning. The popularity of the lectionary has grown. In a recent poll, 70 percent of United Methodist pastors regularly used the lectionary in planning for worship and preaching.[8]

The advantages are compelling. The lectionary permits long-range planning and coordination of worship by pastor, musicians, and worship committees. Major portions of scripture are covered in a systematic way and are also coordinated with the church year. And finally, with the growing acceptance of the common lectionary, there is an abundance of published aids for preaching and worship.

---

[7]Andy Langford, "The Revised Common Lectionary 1992: A Revision for the Next Generation," *Quarterly Review* 13 (Summer 1993): 37–48; and Horace T. Allen, Jr., "Lectionaries–Principles and Problems: A Comparative Analysis," *Studia Liturgica* 22 (1992): 68–83. For another perspective, see Marjorie Procter-Smith, "Lectionaries–Principles and Problems: Alternative Perspectives," *Studia Liturgica* 22 (1992): 84–99; and idem, "Beyond the New Common Lectionary: A Constructive Critique," *Quarterly Review* 13 (Summer 1993): 49–58.

[8]Langford, "The Revised Common Lectionary 1992: A Revision for the Next Generation," 37.

Rediscovery of the Eucharist

The rediscovery of the eucharist is twofold. First, there is the recovery of the concept of "eucharist," of thanksgiving and joy with the Lord's supper that was present in the early church—the idea that worship is a celebration of the risen Christ, present with his people, reconnecting his body, revitalizing his body, restoring his body. Part of the joy of eucharist is the focus on God's action and Christ's mysterious presence through this sacrament rather than on the worshiper's contrition and remembering a bloody cross. Second, with these theological shifts have come a recovery of the more frequent celebration of the eucharist on the Lord's Day. Although many churches have a way to go to realize fully the early church's model of weekly eucharist, denominations that celebrated infrequently are now celebrating bi-weekly or monthly.

An Emphasis on the Vernacular and Cultural Context

Vatican II brought about a radical change when it replaced Latin in the mass with the language of the people, the vernacular. Protestant churches also began to think about the language used in its prayers and hymns. Much of it was archaic, filled with "thee's" and "thou's," and was exclusive, rather than inclusive. ("Man" was used when "human being," rather than "adult male," was meant.) The newer liturgies contain language that better reflects the common usage. Another issue being discussed in churches, given the cultural context of today, is the theological adequacy of using male pronouns for God. Music is still another area gaining prominence in church discussions, and it directly relates to each one's cultural context. Developing and including music that reflects the cultural mix of most churches and that expresses an appropriate theology is a challenge. Many churches solve this problem by creating a variety of worship services with different types of music. Yet, many theologians find this practice troubling, since it undermines the unity of the body of Christ. On a practical level, many churches are too small to run several services. But expanding the types of music in the service to include the cultural and generational diversity is an option open to most churches today. Diversity of music in a single service would also reflect the unity and diversity present in the body of Christ.

Rediscovery of Other Christian Traditions

In the past thirty years, denominational leaders and scholars of different Christian traditions have been talking with one another and learning from one another. Scholars from different traditions, studying the same ancient documents, read one another's articles and attend conferences together, resulting in a cross-fertilization.

Perhaps most important for Protestants and Roman Catholics has been the rediscovery of the Orthodox tradition, which continues to this day many of the worship practices of the early church. The Orthodox view worship as being transported into the heavens with the risen, triumphant Christ and being surrounded by the great cloud of witnesses. The Orthodox have also maintained the use of the *epiclesis,* which dropped out of use in the West. The Orthodox have held on to a clear notion of the community of faith as the body of Christ, believing that it is only through the community of faith, the church, that one is saved; one cannot be saved alone. The Orthodox have retained worship practices that involve the whole person, rather than the Protestant tradition, which uses only the ear. Another arena for ecumenical dialogue is the Commission on Faith and Order of the World Council of Churches. Faith and Order developed the "BEM," or "Baptism, Eucharist, and Ministry," document. This document, created in the representative body and then sent to the various denominations for comment, has helped the various church communions see what they have in common as well as where their theologies and practices differ.

An Emphasis on Proclamation and Social Involvement

As a result of Vatican II, the Roman Catholic Church has recovered the importance of the service of the Word. Now a worship service must have the proclamation of the gospel as well as the service of the table. So Roman Catholics have recovered the service of the Word as Protestants have recovered the service of the table.

Ironically, worship renewal has clarified the boundaries of who is in the church and who is outside it. This is the result of the understanding that in baptism one becomes part of the body of Christ and that weekly worship reconnects and invigorates one as part of the body of Christ. Therefore, the joy one experiences with the risen Christ and his body in worship is an impetus for intercession, witness, and caring. Worship becomes the energizing source for reaching out beyond the walls of the church. With the now acknowledged centrality of the ministry of the laity, the primary evangelism and ministry to society is not by ministers and priests, but by the people. The worship service informs through the proclamation and feeds through the eucharist. A well-known example of this rhythm of worship that leads to reaching out to others, that leads to renewal in worship and then reaching out again, was Mother Teresa of Calcutta.

She began each day with worship in community and then went out to serve the poor and unwanted.

Preaching in Church Renewal

The renewal of worship during the past thirty years has changed preaching in many churches. Worship is now in partnership with preaching rather than the stage and setting for the sermon. One way of strengthening the partnership is to coordinate the lections with the prayers, music, and hymns. The whole worship service, rather than just the sermon, is a proclamation of the Word.

The "new" location of the sermon fosters the integration of the sermon within the service. Rather than at the end, the sermon is centrally located at a pivotal point. The order of worship now allows for a response to the Word in worship. While the revival service allowed for a response to the Word, the response was limited and focused on the "unsaved" and the "backslider." The worship here focuses on the gathered body of Christ, and the response is broadened to include the faithful's encountering Christ in new and deeper ways.

There is the proclaimed Word and the enacted Word. The enacted Word is ideally the Lord's supper. However, on Sundays in those churches that do not have weekly communion, the enacted Word is at least the offering and the prayers of the people. Other responses may include baptism, baptismal renewal, a healing service, the reception of new members, an altar call, and so forth.

Preaching in this order of service requires preaching for a response, not only in actions outside the church, but also in actions within the rest of the service. Remember, the model is Luke 24, and it is through an action that Christ is known, not in the speaking. The opening up of scripture sets the stage for the encounter with Christ, but the words are not the encounter. It is in the response that Christ is known. Therefore, preaching in the context of worship is preaching for a response to the proclaimed Word. The worship is designed so that there will be a response made through the enacted Word. Preaching so that a response will be in the context of worship allows the response to be one of the "community," and not just an individual response outside the worshiping community. The response is an action by the people such as prayer, giving, reciting an affirmation of belief, or some other liturgical action. This responsive action supports the worship renewal's characterization of greater "participation" by the laity. Preaching then becomes more than the transmission of a good idea; it points to a response, and the design of worship provides for the community's initial response.

Of course, following the early church model, the fullest response is the Lord's supper or eucharist. However, I have visited many churches where this is an appendage and not an integral part of worship and where there seems to be no relationship with the proclaimed Word and the enacted Word. Part of the problem is our limited understanding of communion as only that the cross and the shed blood ratify our sins as forgiven, rather than the early church's understanding of it as an encounter with the risen Christ, of eucharist's nourishing us by the bread of heaven, of eucharist's being the medicine of the soul given to us by the Great Physician. The eucharist as an encounter with Christ who makes all things new, who brings new life from death, offers greater possibilities for the Lord's supper to be, in fact, the enacted Word as well as the proclaimed Word. This would allow for a richer "recovery of eucharist."

The "rediscovery of the Bible" through the use of the lectionary raises two distinct issues. One is how to use the lectionary for preaching in the worship service. The second, related issue is how to use the church year in preaching, since the lections are related to the seasons of the church year. Fred Craddock has often said that preaching from a text on Good Friday is different from preaching from that text on Easter. While this is an extreme example, the church calendar does shape the proclamation and the design of the worship service. One frequent abuse of the lectionary is preaching one point from each lection, ignoring the psalms, and therefore having a three-point sermon, often with little relationship between the points. Although the lections are related in some seasons, there are seasons when there is little or no relationship among the different lections. The underlying assumption in this form of preaching is that unless the scripture is used in the sermon, it should not be in the worship service. This goes back to the old understanding that the worship service is the setting for the sermon and that the scripture read is for the sermon. The early church believed that the word of God as revealed in the scriptures was alive. It did not require a preacher to enliven them. Therefore, scripture that is amplified through the prayers and the hymns does not need to be amplified also by the preacher. The preacher needs to preach primarily from one text and, furthermore, to limit what is said about that text to one major idea and the response of the community of faith to that idea. However, many Protestant churches kill the living Word by reading it poorly in worship. The Roman Catholic Church and the Episcopal Church train lay readers. There are programs available to train laity to read a living Word, not a dead one. In the early church, scripture was read aloud because not everyone could have their own parchment or papyrus copy. So the scriptures were created to be read aloud in worship.

One of the ways we learn about ourselves is to encounter ideas or cultures that are different from our own. Many churches include a variety of ethnicities and cultures. A number of denominations are forming special partnerships with other denominations. Occasionally having a worship service that uses music from another culture or tradition with a response from that culture or tradition begins to help the congregation understand in new ways the inclusive nature of God's love and the diversity present in the church, the body of Christ. "Rediscovery of other Christian traditions" builds up the church. Explanation about the special service may be in the announcements, in the children's moment, or perhaps in a newsletter. Preaching on these special Sundays is still proclamation of the good news, based on the scripture with a liturgical response.

Worship that equips the laity for ministry requires preaching that not only touches the hearts and minds of the congregants personally, but also enables them to move beyond the walls of the church to the outside world. This requires preaching for empowerment. This is not "Let us do…" or "We should do…" preaching, because this type of moralistic preaching ignores the risen Christ. The energy "to do…" is from the individual person, is exhausting, and leads to burnout. Empowerment preaching paints a picture of what is possible through the power of Christ's spirit, proclaims the power of God's word to bring forth life from death, and conveys the embracing love of God to uphold and strengthen one for the journey. The issues of our day cannot be ignored. However, the preaching is not "what we must do," but "what God can do with and through us."

The renewal of worship brings new possibilities for preaching. Preaching is now in partnership with the worship service, and scripture is proclaimed throughout the service in the responsive readings, music, and prayers. The spoken word now leads to an enacted Word. The enacted Word involves the whole person, not just the ear and mind, responding to the word of God. The enacted Word involves the community responding, not just the individual. Laity not only get a spiritual boost but also are empowered for ministry.

In the African American church there is a saying that "God makes a way when there is no way." God makes a way for the church to be renewed and strengthened through its proclaimed and enacted Word.

2

ALTAR-ING THE WORLD:
Community-forming Word and Worship

Heather Murray Elkins

The origin of this essay's title is a midsummer class in Word and worship. We were lazily working our way through the classic rhythms of Word-centered traditions of worship. "Altar call," I invited. The response to the call was a chilly silence. "Altar call," I declared. More silence, then revelation: "This is _____(unnamed seminary with impeccable credentials). We don't do those here."

"We don't do those here" is a manifesto of war, a controversy of liturgical/nonliturgical, spirit-filled/textually grounded, high/low, ecumenical/evangelical worship. Just as a prayer book is evidence of the absence of the Holy Spirit to some communions, the practice of having an altar call is the proof of unrepentant revivalism to others. Here is the line in the sand, which all our ecumenical negotiations have not erased.

I meet the challenge head-on. I was raised a child of mountain religion, undereducated, sacramentally deprived, and lacking in table manners, to say the least. Kodachrome colors of country churches flash before my eyes, linked together by circuit-riding pastors who served without the benefit of living wages or seminary. Until recently, local pastors in my tradition were barred from leading prayers at the Lord's table. Given authority only for the Word, they presided at Sunday sacraments of preaching and music, sustained by the reality described in Vatican II's *Constitution on the Sacred Liturgy* as the "real presence of Christ" in the reading and the hearing of the Word.

The sacrament of holy communion was a solemn occasion, linked with the work of the quarterly conference. Those with authority and formal education led the prayers. There was a call to the altar, but only the saints among us dared to kneel and be fed. Eating at this altar could lead to damnation, the preachers warned; let the wise beware.

The joyful table of the Risen One was not located in the sanctuary, but in the fellowship hall or the grassy lot beside the church graveyard. After the singing and preaching were over, a holy and very human form of dining came in the potluck dinners and homecoming feasts, prepared as a foretaste of the heavenly banquet. The shape of these liturgies had a classic dimension: the communion of saints, the forgiveness of sins, the prayers for, and gossip about, the living, and the refrain "Lord, have mercy."

These images, flashes of insight, are sensed as a defense for "altar calls." Class and race and region and gender and economics and the "pure meanness" of human sin bar us from the oneness that Christ commands. What I said in response to "We don't do those here" was what I meant: "Spell it *altar* or *alter*, but if you don't do it, don't preach."

The blunt conviction has not mellowed, but sharpened over the years. It is in the process of altar-ing the world that "the special synergy between God's action and human action occurring in the liturgical act constitutes the horizon of possibility for worship."[1] All liturgical life, preaching, prayer, praise, and service, encompassed in the altar/alter call of Christ. The pain of our divided house of prayer, the shame of our closed communions, are the sharp goads of the Spirit calling us to overturn our tabled agendas so that we may worship in the spirit and truth that God wills. Reasoned disagreements over issues of form and freedom are essential, but the heart of the call comes through communing with the saints, preaching to raise the dead, and feeding the lambs.

My summer revelation of the worthiness of a marginalized community's life of worship is what Margaret Miles calls *theoria*, a term describing the change in perception that accompanies a shift in the sense or meaning of an experience. This is being "lifted out of one's familiar world and into the living presence of the spiritual world" by a concentrated seeing.[2] This insight persists long after the moment

[1] Alceste Catella, "Theology of the Liturgy," in *Handbook for Liturgical Studies,* vol. 2, *Fundamental Liturgy,* ed. Anscar J. Chupungco (Collegeville, Minn.: Liturgical Press, 1998), 9.
[2] Margaret Miles, *Image as Insight: Visual Understanding in Western Christianity and Secular Culture* (Boston: Beacon Press, 1987), 150.

of revelation is over. The evocative implications of the phrase "altar-ing the world" appear in countless encounters of worshiping congregations with the transformative power of the Holy Spirit. This hunger for transformation is the work of faith. This faith is never static; it is not, as Abraham Heschel writes, "clinging to a shrine, but an endless pilgrimage of the heart. Audacious longing, burning songs, daring thoughts, an impulse overwhelming the heart, usurping the mind,– these are all a drive toward Him who rings our hearts like a bell."[3]

To altar is to lift up the commonplace of human life for holy use. To come to Christ's table is a response to an altar call. To resist the economic injustices of a consuming culture in the public square is a response that alters daily life. To provide meals and lodging for a family who visits a son in prison altars a neighborhood. To participate in the release of captives every Sunday alters a congregation.

The Old English word *weorthscipe* provides a code for the grammar of Christian worship: *weorth* (worthy) and *-scipe* (-ship); to attribute worth to another; to esteem another's being. This term provides a primary language for this work of mystagogy, the teaching of the mysteries of God in Christ. One might ask what homiletical common sense can be achieved when the work is *mysterion?* All who practice the art of liturgical preaching struggle with the weekly task of communing and communicating what finally cannot be said. Those who teach the mysteries of Christ, particularly those who write essays, recognize the wisdom of the ancient church's injunction of silence. Yet the sacramental life and language of the community of the Risen One depend on the work of interpreters who break the silence and assist the community in the gradual incorporation of new believers.

For this work of interpretation, I propose four principles to clarify a synergistic approach to Christian preaching and worship. The first principle of altar-ing the world is *the Word of God as sound;* the second, *story as structure;* the third, *image as insight;* and the fourth, *sacrament as alter/altar call.* This four-square approach to the Word of God rests on the affirmation that the Word is the creating and redeeming activity of God in relationship to humanity; revealed in Christ; proclaimed in the church by scripture, sermon, and witness; encountered in the sacraments; and made alive in our hearts by the Holy Spirit. As the *Constitution on the Sacred Liturgy* demonstrates, "The Word is of course sacrament; the sacrament, on the other hand, is an actuation of the

---

[3]Abraham J. Heschel, *I Asked for Wonder: A Spiritual Anthology,* ed. Samuel H. Dresner (New York: Crossroad, 1983), 15.

Word."[4] This approach to Word and *weorthscipe* assumes the creative and redemptive unity of preaching and liturgy. The essential insights of these principles arise from a narrative that will, as they say in the mountains, "set things right."

Word as Sound

This alter/altar call is first sounded in the Hebrew term *dabar*, as recounted in the Genesis event of the Holy One's Spirit/breath moving across "the face of the deep." In the language of the gospel of John, this holy yet fully human Word is named "Jesus the Christ" and is experienced as the Risen One of God. The sense of the gospel in the early church was a sense of sound. Sermons, parables, and poetry mix and mingle in the ancient texts. A line from a favorite hymn, a pun, a prayer, and the rhetorical questions of Jesus are inscribed on the community's memory through the oral recitation of these forms.

Orality, not literacy, shaped the early community's perception of Word and worship. The scriptural texts read in public worship required the sound of the human voice in order to be complete. The saying of a thing was the doing as well: the physicality of an apostolic letter being unrolled and read, the experience of singing in one voice, breathing with one breath, blessing one God. This involved *perception,* the sensing, and making sense, of objects and subjects. This embodied language made a lasting impression on holy and human forms of communication.

A blessing blessed. An excommunication affected one's eternal condition. This is performative language, language that does what it says. Those who were not yet baptized were excluded from the prayers of the people. The affirmation of faith, "Jesus is Lord," was raised over the waters of one's baptism, the time and place of one's death, burial, and resurrection in Christ.

The liturgical practice of making "covenant" remains embedded in the structures of Christian worship, despite the shift from orality to literacy during the Reformation and the present iconic/electronic reformations of human knowledge. This premodern dimension of "Word as sound" continues to form communities of worship, particularly in traditions that are nontextual in their liturgical practice. The call/response of preacher and people, computer-generated hymns and images, praise choruses, and dance choirs are forms of incorporation, designed to teach a new generation to sing with one heart, body, and breath.

---

[4]Catella, "Theology of the Liturgy," 13.

The symbolic-media world of a community such as Taizé surrounds the worshipers with sound, a heightened sense of human solidarity and holiness created partly through congregational singing in Latin, a language whose appeal is heightened by its arcane function. Reading scripture with attentive silence is proclamation. The teaching of scripture takes place in small groups before and after the services: first, participation in the mystery, then comprehension. How it *feels* is the first level of involvement. What it *means* is the second.

We are the progeny of the Protestant Reformation, but we scarcely sense the magnitude of our inheritance. The explosive aftermath of hearing the Word in the vernacular or the ability to read scripture outside the vested authority of the clergy are now matters of footnotes, not faith. This sense-making, community-forming language, however, continues to alter human experience within the Christian community precisely because it is not Word alone; it is sacrament as well.

> If even religious language in our culture is used to lie and to sell and to garner power, like the old moneychangers and merchants in the temple (cf. Mk. 11:15–17), the use of bath and table next to the words intends to overturn the tables in the house of language, rebuilding words themselves as a house of God for all people.[5]

Story as Structure

The immense appeal of narrative can be documented in countless books on preaching as well as on the backs of cereal boxes. A story sells. Even the growing popularity of the Christian year and the increasingly common use of the lectionary can be described in terms of the attraction of "telling time" through the story of Jesus.

What do the stories of Jesus and the community of the Risen One require? Quality time, for starters. Time for the telling. Time for the sharing. Time to learn to tell time in light of the incarnation. Being willing to risk making contact with the story, to let it get under our skin, requires an openness difficult to sustain in the face of the the addictive rhetoric of the marketplace.

The stories of God require those who know the stories by *heart*. A congregation, like a child, asks that we not only read a story, but that we tell a story. In his monumental work *Time and Narrative,*

---

[5]Gordon W. Lathrop, *Holy Things: A Liturgical Theology* (Minneapolis: Fortress Press, 1993), 102.

Paul Ricoeur notes that the only human time is narrated time.[6] It appears that holy time is story time too.

> Here, the word is not just talk; drink the cup with this community and hear what the cup says of God and the hope for God's world. Here, "Jesus" is not just a name from the past, capable of being used for whatever purpose the speaker chooses; this bread given to you *is* who he is. And Israel's story is not just an ancient account of liberation; this bath is that account come to you.[7]

A story is an invitation to cross a threshold, to enter a space where the tyranny of time is held at bay. A story of the good news asserts the power of memory over the forces of amnesia. Our experience of human loneliness can be told within a community shaped by the narrative of the Human One, and in the lyric telling, the fractures between lived time and cosmic time can be bound together. By telling the stories of the beloved Child of God, we bear witness that love is stronger than death. Such stories give us a way to reclaim a lost time or place or presence, particularly the presence of those whom we love. We need a story of the beloved as well as the witness of the Spirit, and we, strengthened by story and Spirit, will be with the world loved by God.

We tell stories as a means of sanctifying time, of shaping relationships. We tell stories as a way of remembering into the future. To tell a gospel story, however, *re-members* us, reconnects us to the presence of the Risen One. In the telling, we reclaim our identity as disciples and friends. In the hearing, we are transformed by the Spirit. In the showing, God's will is done, on earth as it is in heaven.

A story is a temporary structure of human consciousness, but a story can also possess a force field that will alter human history. Why did the world powers of Jesus' day conspire against a man who told stories? What was the source of his power, the force of his threat? A handful of (more or less) nonviolent, underemployed misfits? His economic strength? He had to borrow everything: boats, food, lodgings, taxes. How did he threaten an empire except by his presence and his stories? The man from Nazareth told stories so dangerous to the principalities that they broke their own laws in order to silence him.

---

[6]Paul Ricoeur, *Time and Narrative,* 3 vols. (Chicago: University of Chicago Press, 1988), vol 1, 99.
[7]Lathrop, *Holy Things,* 110.

Narrative preaching is now the height of pulpit fashion. Perhaps essays on narrative theology should be labeled "Warning! Attempting to follow these principles may prove hazardous to your health." There are, have been, and will be tellers of dangerous stories of joy. Those who have been gifted and burdened with the paradoxical authority of pastoral office are servants of the Word, servers at the table, bound by the unique mystery of Christ and God's history of salvation. The telling of these mysteries, this history, is located in the particular times and places of worshiping congregations. We inherit not only the gospel stories from our ancestors, but also their intonations, their liturgical shapes, their gestures. We are *traditioned* by these stories within our worshiping traditions, and the shaping of our individual and corporate identities are deeply connected to these shared narratives. In constructing a discipline of preaching or liturgical leadership within a community of interpreters, we discovered that it is scripture that interprets us:

> Our life situation will necessarily determine the questions we bring to the text, and hence strongly influence what it says and means to us. At the same time, the text maintains its integrity, and we owe it to ourselves and the text to try to enter into its world as much as possible. Then, if we are genuinely listening to the text, we will allow it to influence how we understand and what we do about our situation (it "interprets" us).[8]

The ethical implications of a shared narrative require critical attention on the part of preachers, practitioners, and teachers of the Christian community. What we revere as holy can assume profane dimensions. Tradition can lead to idolatry, the antithesis of the esteeming of the being of God and the other. The traditional reading of the narratives for Good Friday is linked to a painful history of anti-Semitism; therefore, a word of caution is inserted into *The Handbook of the Christian Year*, giving the motivation for the change of the text: religious authorities/Jews.

> They [the Reproaches] ask questions that reveal our own rebellion and complicity in the sufferings of Christ and in the evil and sufferings in the world. Images from scripture are used concerning Israel and God's hand in that holy

---

[8]Ched Myers, *Binding the Strong Man: A Political Reading of Mark's Story of Jesus* (Maryknoll, N.Y.: Orbis Books, 1988), 5.

history, but the accusations are clearly aimed at the faithless-
ness of all who would call upon God...The accusations are
like an inversion of the holy history we recite and recall in
the Great Thanksgiving at the Lord's table.[9]

These narratives, these concepts, these forms of liturgical life are inseparable from the reality of our lives in Christ. Life versus liturgy is
a false distinction, and the fierce condemnation of unworthy worship
by the prophet Amos should warn us against such divisions. "The
difference between the cultic mystery and the real mystery that is
Christ lies only in the fact that the former is the symbolic representa-
tion of the latter; therefore the difference involves only the mode of
being, not the essence itself of the mystery."[10]

The primary telling of the "holy history" that links the preaching
and the sacramental lives of a congregation can be located in a few
key texts of the Lord's table: Matthew 26:26–30; Luke 22:14–23;
Mark 14:22–25; and 1 Corinthians 11:23–26. These are the critical
narratives of God's self-giving, the life of the sacraments, and the
sacraments of life. Key theological concepts that these narratives have
engraved in the structures of Christian life and liturgy are those of
sacrifice, thanksgiving, mystery, resurrection of the body, forgiveness of sin, justice, memorial, and the eschatological promise of a
new creation.

In his book *Congregations: Stories and Structures*,[11] James Hopewell
relies on the work of Northrop Frye[12] to expand the implications of
congregational narratives: tragic, comic, romantic, ironic. The
relationship between preaching and worship is formed by a narrative that is chosen by the community for its own self-telling. That
self-telling is rarely self-aware, however, and is never literalistic.
Compare the following words of institution: "On the night in which
he gave himself up for us...," and "On the night in which he was
betrayed..." Both are authorized texts for the United Methodist Service of Word and Table. The horizon of meaning that each narrative
has reveals such distinct patterns of prayer and theology that they
constitute separate universes residing within the same tradition. It

[9]Hoyt L. Hickman, Don E. Saliers, Laurence Hull Stookey, and James F. White,
eds., *The New Handbook of the Christian Year* (Nashville: Abingdon Press, 1992), 190.
[10]Catella, "Theology of the Liturgy," 12.
[11]James F. Hopewell, *Congregations: Stories and Structures* (Philadelphia: Fortress
Press, 1987).
[12]Northrop Frye, *Anatomy of Criticism* (Princeton, N.J.: Princeton University Press,
1957).

might even be possible to predict that too selective a use of one narrative will diminish the diverse symbolic and social world of that tradition.

Delores Williams' essay "Rituals of Resistance in Womanist Worship"[13] expands this concept of an organic relationship between story/scripture/sermon/sacrament. A community's relationship to scripture and its authority-claim on the patterning of worship is critical for the community's sense of worth. What story is told and how the telling takes place create the particularities of a community's worship. The vital interplay recorded in oral traditions of scripture constantly reconstructs holy text from human context.

> First, early Christian origins for the black community were in the early slave period of African-American history. That was when they began fashioning a world view out of the biblical images and stories they selected as appropriate to their life situation—the biblical material that spoke the good news in male and female terms. That is when and how their testimonies, songs, and narratives say they met Jesus.[14]

The community's liturgical inclusion of a holy text beyond the printed text is a tradition in many international Christian communities. Testimonies of local saints with their patterned language of suffering and the advent of deliverance belong to the unwritten order of worship. These oral traditions can sustain a community when aggressive cultural and market forces of globalization destabilize inherited patterns of religious meaning. Its continuing worth is the way it can liberate a congregation from pulpit domination or the restrictive use of scripture. This is a worship principle that, in practice, hallows a marginalized community's experience and sustains the memory of God's particular grace in this particular place.

Image as Insight

> "Mystery," indeed, is the historical unfolding of the salvation worked by God in Christ; in the "meantime" the Church lives in the faith and in the mystery of the worship of Christ.[15]

---

[13]Delores S. Williams, "Rituals of Resistance in Womanist Worship," in *Women at Worship: Interpretations of North American Diversity*, ed. Marjorie Procter-Smith and Janet R. Walton (Louisville, Ky.: Westminster/John Knox Press, 1993), 215–23.

[14]Ibid., 222.

[15]Catella, "Theology of the Liturgy," 8.

It was not an ideal setting for a Christmas play. A narrow space between a wall of concrete block and the first row of benches served as the stage. The lighting was simple: on or off. The costumes were less than homemade: a football jersey, burlap and twine, scruffy blankets, prison uniforms worn inside out and upside down. The cast was uneven, to say the least. One actor claimed a master's degree. One could not read and had to learn his part, line by line, recited by a buddy two cells down. Less than ideal, more eloquently than a sermon could convey, this real-life, hard-time drama cured me forever of wanting fur on the wise men's robes. The gospel arrives, wrapped in clean rags every time.

The prison regulations prevented me from bringing in "good" costumes. This initial frustration meant that the ordinary stuff of a very bare human environment became the "evidence of things not seen." It also taught me an essential lesson about preaching for a particular people in a certain time and place. By assuming the limitations, taking on the particulars, the essential theological identity of the Christian community as an incarnational presence is revealed.

A blanket with holes is a cause for complaint. A ragged shepherd's cloak is a realistic prop for a novice actor. A prison yard is a desolate place, spare of grass and grace. A prison yard is an ideal Bethlehem scene, with graying walls of stone, hard ground, and the smell of occupation. No need to imagine a cast of Roman guards. They remained in place on the walls, keeping watch over their flock by day and by night. Just as God assumed the limitations of a "stiff-necked" human race, so a wealth of grace resides in the poverty of place.

"In the beginning was the Word," and that was the heart of the problem. I could not find a Christmas script that fit. What works in a misty-eyed tradition of Norman Rockwell's Christmas Eve or in a postmodern narrative minimalist tradition did not work here. A maximum security prison is a world of its own, needing a language as brutal and sophisticated as its own life, or, as one of the guards explained it, "My perception is your reality." What word could be called "gospel" and become flesh in this place?

From a barely remembered assignment in sophomore English, I recovered *The Second Shepherd's Play,* from a medieval dramatic genre named, aptly enough, a mystery play. Composed in a time when shepherds stood one step above slaves and one foot outside the law, it had a familiar ring to men who recited a number before they could say their name. The rhymed couplets were a bit much, though the yard rap had its own charm.

I told them the story. They listened. I told it again. They questioned it, turned it over, checked its strength, then told me what they knew. I listened. Word by word we reconstructed this "make-believe" so it would belong to their place, their hard time.

One prisoner was so taken by this "make-believe" that he insisted on changing the end of the story. He played the thief who steals the lamb, disguising himself as a woman in labor. His disguise works until the shepherds recognize the voice of the lamb, hidden under his skirt/shirt. Only the arrival of Joseph and a very expectant Mary prevents his hanging.

In the original version, the thief disappears as soon as he's set free, leaving the shepherds to honor the newborn messiah. This particular thief/prisoner insisted on a rewrite. He wanted to return the lamb himself to honor the Christ child. He demanded to be allowed to kneel beside the shepherds. He refused to be left "out in the cold." When I pressed for a reason, it came: This king, this king doesn't mind a thief hangin' 'round.

We needed a prop, a lamb small enough to hide under a shirt, yet big enough to resemble the animal. The theft of this creation is the heart of the play. I gave the assignment like a mission impossible. Required: one lamb. No questions asked, no prisoners taken.

It was ready for inspection the following week. The lead shepherd laid it on the table in the visitation room for inspection. He waited for a verdict. I was properly amazed. The lamb consisted of:

- a cardboard box covered with cotton balls (medical supplies?)
- ears and tail from a pillow case
- a head made from a navy-blue stocking cap (the donor risked below-freezing temperatures every day, all day in the yard)
- four white socks for legs.

The socks caught my attention. They were blatantly new. The explanation of their whiteness and their acquisition had sparked the conception of the lamb. Prisoners were issued new socks twice a year. Four prisoners, nonperformers, had each donated one sock, so that no one would be short something new. Every time I crossed the yard, I looked at the clusters of men in the yard and wondered which four wore one "holy" sock.

The notion of a sacrificial lamb gained strength every time I looked at their creation. The men named the prop "Chops" and made jokes about its pieced-together appearance. As weeks of rehearsal passed, I noticed that they each took turns holding the lamb while the others rehearsed. These were grown men guilty of terrible crimes. They had stories I did not want to know. That stark reality was gradually overlaid with an alternative vision: small boys, sitting alone, rocking and hugging a long-lost toy.

The prop began to move and have a symbolic life beyond its function, beyond its plotline. Lamb of God. So obvious. So new. Its presence created a tension fed by the absence of another object, the baby Jesus. No child was permitted in this violent space. No doll was allowed through the gate, but its lack was a blessing. What color eyes, what color face could express the vision of Christ?

We practiced with an empty manger (cardboard box, shoe-polished sides), but the absence was oppressive. The emptiness seemed like a lie, a collapse of "make-believe." What could serve as the means of grace, the evidence of "God with us," Immanuel?

The answer was literally off the wall. "Mary" looked at the lamb held in the arms of a proudly penitent thief and walked into the chaplain's office. "She" reentered the chapel with something wrapped in a towel. Human beings can turn an object into a symbol, an action into a rite. The rehearsal suddenly took on the tension of a sacrament, *mysterium*. What had been hidden? What would be revealed? When the time came, the cloth was removed and its mystery lifted: a crucifix. No one said a word. For the longest time, no one said a thing. *Theoria:* "Behold the Lamb of God that taketh away the sins of the world."

Sacraments as Altar/Alter Call

Human consciousness is not a static condition, but a process of binding things together. Our perceptions of truth and meaning are essentially the perceptions of connections, relationships. These relationships include the verbal processing of reality, ritual gestures, sense perceptions, dreaming, singing, reading, creating order, resisting bodily control. The word "ceremony" derives its meaning from the Latin *caerimonia*, to bind back together that which is separate. In a ceremonial act we are expressing our wonder at the mystery of existence; we rely on visionary images to accomplish the purpose of binding the known to the unknown, the past with the future.

The ceremonial actions of the sacraments bind individual bodies and lives together in a communion of saints. It is not simply an exercise or process that one experiences briefly or only intellectually. Conversion demands that there be an entirely new way of being, "an attitude that sets us against the social set-up of our time."[16]

I carried the memories of the prison lamb and crucifix as if they had literally been impressed against my skin. Here was insight that

---

[16]Leonardo Boff, *Sacraments of Life, Life of the Sacraments* (Washington: D.C.: Pastoral Press, 1987), 79.

transformed the traditional Christmas text into a gospel of liberation. Here was a narrative that could set captives free. The experience, however, would be seen as violating the ceremonial life of the congregation. To tell a story of a criminal who cross-dressed as Mary would be heard as profanity, desecrating Christmas.

Some members had objected to my presence in the prison, period. Some disguised their rejection of the experience by complaining of my absence from the parish. I knew that for most the crisis of incorporating that narrative in the presence of the sacrament would be memorable. No communion was possible between prisoners and parishioners because no communication was permitted. The bodies and the stories of these two communities were constrained to remain separate. Criminals did not belong in the sanctuary. The traditional service of candlelight, carols, and holy communion told the life of this congregation as they wished it to be. They would, if asked, refuse to alter either the story or the traditional symbols, such as a festival of holiday food in the narthex designed to sustain this congregation's sense of body. As Mary Douglas points out:

> The human body is always treated as an image of society...
> The social body constrains the way in which the physical body is perceived. The physical experience of the body, always modified by the social categories through which it is known, sustains a particular view of society.[17]

The rule of thumb for liturgical preparation for this particular body of Christ was to prepare to feed the five thousand. Some forms of hospitality were never practiced, however. No racial lines were ever crossed. There were prison connections within a family, but no one, to my knowledge, ever visited the prison.

Conversion requires an entirely new way of being. Once the world has been *altared,* the ceremonial life of a community will change. As I reflect on this essay, I cannot say if it was the Christmas story, the sermon, or the crucifix borrowed from the chaplain that transformed the community. Was it the cup of forgiveness, the homemade bread, or the gospel that opened their homes? God knows. What matters is that their stories and structures were transformed after that Christmas Eve service. Just as a personal story dramatizes the community's sense of self and its world, the personal bodies of a congregation can measure theological understanding. This community's *weorthscipe*

[17]Mary Douglas, *Natural Symbols: Explorations in Cosmology* (London: Routledge, 1996), 99.

structure could be witnessed in their bodily transformations. The ceremonial recitation of a story about captives made its connection to a congregation who believed themselves to be free men and women. Prison visitations began, books were gathered, letters started. Release was proclaimed to the captives, and those who were set free took that liberation into the sanctuary, cell, and public square.

There is no common life, no common ground, no common action without an agreement on the shared story and the common table. When the normal restraints of the social body of a congregation are altered, the physical experience transforms the social categories. A change in bodily actions takes place among individuals whose stories then continue to shape the shared structures of meaning. This is community-forming Word and worship. Our task as presiders and preachers is to assume the limitations, affirm their life in their language, presume prevenient grace, and to remember that symbols require communal nurture to survive. Our identity is that of witness, interpreter, or, as the gospel of Luke puts it:

> Since many have undertaken to set down an orderly account of the events that have been fulfilled among us, just as they were handed on to us by those who from the beginning were eyewitnesses and servants of the word, I too decided, after investigating everything carefully from the very first, to write an orderly account for you...(Lk. 1:1–3)

3

Worship Amplifies the Voice of the Preacher

Robin L. Meyers

Those of us fortunate enough to be students of Charles Rice have always suspected that his pilgrimage from the Baptist Church to the United Church of Christ to the Episcopal Church must have had *something* to do with changing liturgical needs! Although he downplays any conscious connection, it is tempting to believe that on some unconscious level his life is a kind of metaphor for the mysterious and vital connection that this book has adopted as its thesis—namely, that any artificial separation of worship from preaching will ultimately imperil both. His life also shows that the old bromide may be a bit oversimplified: "There are liturgical Christians and there are non-liturgical Christians." Indeed, the truth of that statement may be something closer to the oft-used (perhaps overused) analogy of the left brain and the right brain. Charles Rice taught us that worship and preaching are vital partners in a mysterious kind of integration in which the people of God are made ready to hear and then by grace sometimes *do hear* the word of God.

I share the Reformed roots of my good teacher, in which the sermon was king, and the princes of the pulpit ruled from their elevated thrones. The order of worship was often called a "hymn sandwich," a tongue-in-cheek way of confessing that everything occurring before the sermon was prelude and everything after it was postlude. The liturgy was so sparse that it seemed more like an incantation, a "warm-up" for the main event rather than an integral part of the worship experience. Being called to worship, confessing our sins, reciting the Lord's Prayer, and singing a couple of hymns (pick a hymn, any hymn) was almost like paying our dues, subconsciously,

27

because everyone knows that you can't just start preaching right after the congregation sits down following the opening hymn!

I began my career as an ordained minister twenty years ago feeling practically the same way. I would never have said that I didn't think liturgy was important, because that would have been politically incorrect, but, in fact, I acted as if it didn't really matter. After all, I had the sermon to think about, to get ready, and to get right. Who has time to figure out whether the call to worship sets the right tone, or hymns demonstrate a thematic, or at least seasonal, congruence with the sermon? Who has time to pick the right psalm or to make sure that the closing hymn doesn't turn around and belt out the very theology that the sermon has just called "bad"? The preacher can't do everything, I assured myself. Besides, wouldn't that constitute "rigging" the worship experience, as if people couldn't make their own connections? They might be ministered to by a totally different theme in a hymn with no connection to the sermon but a valid, and in some cases even a profoundly relevant, message.

These are good excuses, but a wise man has reminded us that if we are looking for the umbrella of an excuse to hide under, the beach of the ministry is littered with them. It remains a matter of "rationalized laziness" because the work that is required to make the liturgy and the sermon into a dynamic partnership takes time and energy. It takes a keen understanding of the dynamics of human communication in a spiritual context. And it also takes a fundamental kind of *humility*. We must be humble enough to embrace what is not completely under our control, to look for help wherever help can be found. We must cast the net of the Spirit in an arc much wider than the circumference of the pulpit.

Before we go further, however, let me make sure that there is no misunderstanding. This is not a call to divert energy away from the sermon. I remain convinced that the church suffers most from preaching that lacks passion, authenticity, and courage. Nothing I say is meant to compromise anyone's commitment to the high and difficult art of preaching. Rather, it is a call to consider *saving* some energy for a thoughtful and disciplined approach to the preparation and unfolding of a worship experience. Such a worship experience not only prepares people to hear the Word, but it amplifies the voice of the one who dares to speak it. Every preacher should know that failure to tend to the worship experience affects not only those who sit in the pews, but also removes that vital ecclesiastical scaffolding that holds the preacher above the abyss. Such preparation envelops the sermon in prayer and scripture and a cloud of musical witnesses. In fact, if she is paying attention, the preacher will know the truth, and the truth will set her voice free. Dynamic and integrated worship not only helps the listener, but can literally "clear the preacher's throat."

When I speak of an amplified voice here I'm not talking about volume. Meaningful worship doesn't make the preacher louder, but it does add a certain clarity, depth, and confidence that comes from knowing that one has both a duty and a right to speak. Amplified preaching comes from knowing that the gospel belongs to everyone present. The preacher is not the one whose opinions are canonized, but the one called by the body of Christ to sing the old refrain, even as he supplies new words. It is the clear, strong, unapologetic voice of one who knows that she speaks for an ancient and precious community, and that, as with Jeremiah, God reaches out and "touches the mouth" of those who speak faithfully and fearlessly. Amplified preaching has an unmistakable sound, not in its pitch or tone, or even in its rhetorical flourish, but rather in the "unblinking" way it sounds, as if the voice and the eyes are one, neither gaze nor ear averted.

For example, consider this message and moment in perfect harmony: a loving parent singing a lullaby to a beloved child. The voice comes so easily. No need to practice the scales or worry about how the child is going to react. The act is seamless, the sound is so natural that ordinary concerns about whether this song fits, or whether this is the right time to try "this lullaby" are put aside. The only sound is the unmistakable resonance of love. No lemon water, no throat lozenges, no primal screaming to lower the voice a few octaves (I know a minister who does this)—just the single greatest medicine ever invented to spiritually amplify the voice: *appropriateness*.

It matters very much whether the worship service and the sermon are appropriate partners in the dance of revelation. Harmony results when they are, discord when they are not. I am indebted to my preaching professor, Fred Craddock, for having made the theological case for appropriateness so well in his Lyman Beecher Lectures:

> In short, we are talking about being *appropriate*, appropriate in language, mood, and style to the message, the listeners, the occasion. I surprise myself with the weight of importance I now put upon *fittingness*. It was not always so. Appropriate has to do with what is proper, and in the vigorous enthusiasm of my camel hair and leather girdle days I saw absolutely no kinship between the weighty matters of the faith and concern for what is proper. Our religion is made of

sterner stuff: speak of right or wrong, good or evil, true or false, but not of proper or improper as though our business were to lecture on good manners. But through the intervening years, I have observed the inappropriate. At times it has been comical, as Mary's lamb at school. At other times, painful, as Prince Hamlet felt the inappropriateness of his mother's marriage to his uncle before the flowers had faded on his father's grave. And on occasion, the fragile phrase "out of place" has defined evil. Is not a drug quite often a medicine out of place? Is not Satan an angel out of place? On the other hand, all of us have known the beauty and power and goodness of the appropriate word or card or act or gift. There is unmatched eloquence in the appropriate word.[1]

To this I would add that there is also an unmatched eloquence in the worship service and sermon that work together in appropriate ways. Not only are beauty and power released in the sanctuary, but the voice of the preacher takes on an unmistakable tone, one amplified by all that comes before the sermon and confirmed by all that comes after. The currents of worship do not just wash around the preacher, they carry him along, and when song, prayer, and scripture flood the room, the rising tide really *does* float all boats.

For those of you who are now in seminary, as well as those already in the parish or in other church-related vocations, the question cannot be avoided: What is my responsibility in creating a worship service that is a fitting *partner* with the sermon in the mediation of God's Word? Should we be just as concerned with the hermeneutic of worship as we are with interpreting the text? If our concern is appropriateness, or, to use the old phrase, to do what is "right and meet," what would this look like, sound like, and feel like across different traditions?

Practically speaking, there will always be significant variations in worship style and content as long as there are high and low church traditions and as long as people experiment with new ways to tell the story. The eucharist will always be observed with differing frequencies, and those frequencies will always be defended in ways that indicate respect for the Lord's supper (more often is better; too often becomes rote). Musical styles will always vary according to ethnic

---

[1]Fred B. Craddock, *Overhearing the Gospel* (Nashville: Abingdon Press, 1978), 81.

and cultural traditions, and liturgies will vary as well. But having said this, a case can be made for worship that is *congruent* with preaching and that understands the inseparability of altar and pulpit. I suggest six elements of worship that, when carefully considered, might conspire to amplify the voice of the preacher: communication theory, movement, language, listening, music, and the lectionary.

Communication Theory

An understanding of basic communication theory applies not just to the sermon, but to the entire order of worship. When liturgies are written, when prayers are composed, even when the concerns of the church are shared from the pulpit, a minister has a sacred responsibility to understand how the speaking and hearing of words creates *meaning* in any community. Basic rhetorical theory, and especially the work of Kenneth Burke, can be helpful. For Burke, every rhetorical action is a kind of mini-drama made up of five components: act, scene, agent, agency, and purpose. For this discussion, to speak from the pulpit is the act, the environment of worship is the scene, the preacher is the agent, the actual sermon is the agency, and the purpose is to effect a new hearing of God's Word.

Burke believed that "the scene contains the act" and that "the scene contains the agents." To put it simply: "Language does not possess communicative properties outside the community that authorizes and understands it. The words *communicate* and *community* come from the same root. Language is not neutral with regard to place."[2] With this helpful reminder, Richard Lischer repeats the wisdom of the ages: Whether in worship or in preaching, there are no such things as portable communication or speeches marked "good for any occasion." He reminds us that the "sweet nothings" lovers whisper to each other are not really "nothing" at all. "They are the mutually agreed-upon acts and agencies that have meaning within the narrow confines of the lovers' 'scene,' which is the history of their relationship."[3]

In real estate there is an old adage, "location, location, location." In communication the maxim is context, context, context. To

[2]Kenneth Burke, *A Grammar of Motives* (Berkeley: University of California Press, 1959 [1945]), 3–9.
[3]Richard Lischer, "Preaching as the Church's Language," in *Listening to the Word*, ed. Gail R. O'Day and Thomas G. Long (Nashville: Abingdon Press, 1993), 117.

communicate clearly, forcefully, and faithfully in the context of worship requires not just a careful understanding of the meaning of worship, but a worshipful understanding of the "meaning" of meaning. People bring certain expectations to the sanctuary, certain tolerances; but most of all, they bring certain fundamental needs, and none more palpable than the need to hear a word from God.

Worship should be directed ultimately toward this end. That means that every element of the service is finally a "servant of revelation." It is not primarily about the transfer of information, no matter how important. Nor is it about a socially acceptable display of good intentions or inclinations. It is about opening the heavens to everyone in the sanctuary, including the preacher. Naturally, we begin worship by coming into the sanctuary as if to carry our great secret into our beloved holy space. Here it can most appropriately be shared, because we don't want to keep it to ourselves. God has spoken before; God will speak again; God may be speaking *right now.* All communication during the worship service should be formed around this expectation. Worship should be aimed at moving us from the back of our seats forward. Its principal ingredient should be life's chief pleasure, *anticipation.*

Movement

One of my most common experiences in worship, unfortunately, is to wonder, *Why can't we get on with it?* I don't want to feel this way, but it happens all the time. I go into the sanctuary with high hopes, intending to feel a kind of spiritual vortex. I want to be broken up so that a gospel seed might take root. But with painful regularity other thoughts get in the way; for example, *Why on earth is someone talking about the rummage sale right now? Especially right after that rendition of 'Amazing Grace'? Have we lost our minds?* It's not that the rummage sale is unimportant. It's that talk of the rummage sale doesn't belong here. Announcements (if they must be made at all) should be early, brief, and ever-mindful that a literate congregation can read them. Lifting up the concerns of the parish is one thing, but too often we get a kind of oral bulletin board.

Eugene Lowry has written extensively about the often-neglected element of *time* in the experience of effective preaching. What we are all hoping for is a sermon that "flies" as opposed to one that "crashes."[4]

---

[4]Eugene Lowry, *The Sermon: Dancing the Edge of Mystery* (Nashville: Abingdon Press, 1997), 54.

And that means, of course, that the sermon must "flow." Like any performance in the service of revelation, sermons are bound by the same principles of movement, timing, and conflict/resolution that apply to all art. It is not surprising that Lowry, a jazz pianist, should know something about timing and improvisation. Movement is everything, and timing is no secondary concern, because form and content are inseparable. It is only natural that he would use the word *plot* to describe these crucial concerns in preaching, but in fact the same thing can be said of the worship service. If anyone's heart is to be "strangely warmed" in the sanctuary, then the arteries that lead there must be opened up. Since the truth about preaching is that "impression precedes expression,"[5] something very similar can be said about the listener, namely: Impression precedes *receptivity*.

We begin to build the emotional and spiritual nest into which the words of the service will be dropped when a teenage acolyte strides self-consciously down the center aisle to light the candles: This is holy space. The candle flame is not for lighting cigarettes, and the communion table is not for playing poker.

After the prelude has finished (and hopefully the congregation has used the time to begin the process of being drawn both into and out of themselves), the processional hymn announces that it's time to stand up. After all, if we can do this when a judge enters the courtroom, we can surely do it for the worship of God. Like the one who shouts, "The bridegroom cometh!" the opening hymn rouses us from quiet and individual contemplation and reminds us that something both urgent and collective has begun, something that requires all of our voices.

From this point on, of course, worship services are as varied as the traditions they represent. It is surprising to note how similar their basic elements are. A prayer of *confession* (here's hoping the church is no longer afraid to use that word) usually comes early and establishes something crucial for everyone in the sanctuary: We are *separated*—from God and from one another. We are not as we ought to be, and we need to *say so*. Since appetite precedes insight, as Kierkegaard reminded us, worshipers need to "voice their condition" in order to be made ready for the nourishment that comes in the form of encouragement and pardon. The sequence is not unlike explaining to a physician where it hurts. Symptoms precede diagnosis; this culminates

---

[5]Fred B. Craddock, *As One without Authority* (Enid, Okla.: Phillips University Press, 1974), 80.

in treatment, which ends (we hope) in healing and gratitude–not a bad way to think of the overall movement of Christian worship.

Therefore, prayers of confession (or any kind of prayer written to be read in unison by the congregation) should be brief, straightforward, and possess a humble sort of candor. It's not the time to condemn distant sins or crush the spirit of hopeful worshipers by reminding them of how desperately miserable they are. Rather, it's a time to open with an honest word, to drop all heads and avert all gazes and say to God, in the vernacular: "There, I've gone and said it now...we need to work on me." One of my newest habits is to compose the prayer of confession based on the theme of the sermon, which is usually drawn from the Revised Common Lectionary. Thus, the prayer itself anticipates the sermon and positions the congregation to receive the Word as those who *need* to hear it, not just as those who happen to be hearing it.

Everything in worship is part of a developing crescendo, and it should be allowed to gather speed, emotionally speaking, as we move toward hearing the Word and sharing the risks of interpreting it. Pastoral prayers ought to be specific to *this* congregation, gathering up even the morning's weather, not to mention the dark valleys through which beloved members are passing. It's called a "pastoral" prayer because only the pastor of *that* congregation is qualified to speak it. It requires "local knowledge" of the best kind and requires no apology to those who don't understand it. If they really feel left out of this "insider discourse," let them join the church!

The Lord's Prayer reminds us that the disciples' request ("Lord, teach us to pray") is our request, and the answer cannot be heard too often. Each liturgical element that precedes the sermon, whatever the particular tradition dictates, should anticipate the moment when the text will be read and a "new hearing" will be attempted. The sermon hymn should be contemplative to soften the right side of the brain and bear us away to places beyond the reach of the intellect. Everything is now ready. The worship has prepared us to *hear* the reading of the text, because first and last we are a community shaped by *hearing*. Faith is largely an acoustical phenomenon, and the worship service can be thought of as a song–each verse in different ways prepares us for the refrain. So keep it brief, and keep it moving.

Language

Charles Rice's essay "The Story of Our Times" makes the case for religious language that is not oblivious to the culture that produced it. He opens the essay with these words: "A community tells its story—to itself—as culture."[6] With this reminder Rice brings a helpful critique to a church that is often, as Hans Küng put it, "too busy dusting plastic flowers to cultivate roses." Indeed, it often sounds as if the church is so committed to the avoidance of change that whole generations have failed to hear its message at all. Much of the problem has to do with *language* in both liturgy and sermon.

There is, of course, a healthy tension here. Sometimes our efforts to communicate in the vernacular are little more than shallow efforts at being "hip." For example, the line "Jesus and the boys were whippin' it up down by the sea of Galilee" is heard once too often the first time. Being "relevant" is not to be confused with being cute. Rice wants us to be *real,* and this does not require the church to compromise its message in order to have it be heard. Rather, he urges us to speak in ways that people understand because our listeners are the ones who have helped *create* that way of speaking (and, hence, that way of hearing) to begin with. Dictionaries, I remind my students, are not repositories for the absolute meanings of words. They are the periodic installments that reflect our latest linguistic habits.

Since form and content really are inseparable, we are all justifiably nervous about how to translate our message into meaningful forms without compromising its essential content. Because the church has a distinctive way of talking and with it a distinctive way of calling followers to be in the world, the Bible can provide not just a source for the sermon, but helpful ways of proclaiming it. That's what "biblical" preaching really is, not just sermons peppered with a sufficient number of verses. Thus, preachers walk the tightrope between this world and the world of scripture. We have a faithful desire to carry forward and not compromise the distinctive language of the church. What can keep us from falling?

It helps us to know that the message of the gospel (which *is* a worldview in a sense) has always translated itself into new forms without necessarily losing its essential content. Gail O'Day has written about the church's distinctive message, calling it a "word of hope spoken in the face of fear," the "preaching [of] God's promises in exile," the "*fear not* news of the church," and "preaching as salvation oracle."[7] These essential messages will drive the creation of new

---

[6]Edmund Steimle, Morris Niedenthal, and Charles Rice, *Preaching the Story* (Philadelphia: Fortress Press, 1980), 55.

[7]Gail O'Day, "Toward a Biblical Theology of Preaching," in *Listening to the Word,* 17–32.

language forms to communicate them, even as they insist that the form and the content be compatible. Whether in the sermon or in the creation of a worship service that serves and enhances the sermon, language *matters*. And if we're going to be "biblical" about it, we need to know what that means.

When it comes to the language of the Bible, this very helpful four-part model bears repeating. (1) The Bible addresses the community of faith and is not a collection of theological and ethical arguments to persuade atheists or adherents of other religions. (2) The Bible does not repeat a story verbatim and then from that story draw lessons and exhortations appropriate to the particular audience, but rather retells the story in such a way that it properly addresses the hearers. (3) The Bible addresses particular situations and does not worry about harmonizing each message with all its other messages on that topic. (4) The Bible presents its messages in vivid images, analogies, and metaphors.[8]

If "biblical" preaching is the goal, then what would "biblical" *worship* sound like? It, too, would use "insider discourse" unapologetically and allow the curious to "overhear." It, too, would tell its story in ways that make sense to a particular audience meeting in a particular place and time. It, too, would try to address the concrete concerns of the listener without stopping to interrupt itself continually with assurances that there are other possible options or opinions. "On the other hand" is fine for the coffee shop, but used incessantly in church it drains vitality from both pulpit and chancel. Finally, a "biblical" worship service would also employ language that described more than it "explained" and would be unapologetically poetic–not so that it would sound sophisticated, but so that new images could be hung in the gallery of the mind.

Listening

In my own work, I have come to believe that *deafness* is one of the major causes of bad preaching. I'm not talking about listeners who can't hear. The problem seems to be with preachers who aren't listening! To put it bluntly, "Those who can't hear themselves can hardly expect to be heard."[9] Those who preach are not just called upon to make the right kind of noise, but to produce the right kind of sound. Remember, the sanctuary is not just a safe place; it is also a

---

[8]Craddock, *Overhearing the Gospel,* 65–69.
[9]Robin Meyers, *With Ears to Hear: Preaching as Self-Persuasion* (Cleveland: Pilgrim Press, 1993), 35.

place where people come to escape the world's constant (and often meaningless) racket.

Thus, the sanctuary must be, to begin, a *quiet* space, one in which words and music break the silence because they must–and yet, *carefully*. Good sermons are not so much written as they are "sounded out." The preacher's own ear is the first line of defense against the irrelevant, the obtuse, the peripheral. The same is true of the worship service. It, too, should be "sounded out." Otherwise, things are bound to clash. I have argued that preachers need to "overhear" their own sermons. But the same thing can be said of the "musical score" that is the worship. We are required to ask: Is this liturgy, in any recognizable sense, a "melody," or is it just a "cacophony"? How does the worship service *prepare* people to listen so that the most mysterious and powerful of all possible moments can occur: the vibration of the word of God across human eardrums?

One of the most helpful ways to conceive of a worship service is to remember that it provides the opportunity not just to celebrate and act on our faith, but to set aside an hour in which to sit still and *listen.* Barbara Brown Taylor has written eloquently about the silence of God. She reminds us that the central Jewish declaration of faith is not "I believe," but "Hear, O Israel." "The focus is on the ears, not the lips–on listening, not on speaking."[10] The command to "Be still, and know that I am God" is a definitive command, and this was before pagers and cell phones! Our need to make noise, more or less constantly, and to fear silence and the loss of control that can accompany it, is well known. But in the sanctuary, our failure to listen is often reflected in the rhetoric of the liturgy, especially prayer.

> Our corporate prayers are punctuated with phrases such as "Hear us Lord" or "Lord, hear our prayer," as if the burden to listen were on God and not us. We name our concerns, giving God suggestions on what to do about them. What reversal of power might occur if we turned the process around, naming our concerns and asking God to tell us what to do about them? "Speak, Lord, for your servants are listening."[11]

A worship service that prepared everyone to listen, and thus amplified the voice of the preacher, would begin in silence and then proceed to

---

[10]Barbara Brown Taylor, *When God is Silent* (Boston: Cowley Publications, 1997), 49–50.

[11]Ibid., 50.

the faithful breaking of that silence. That means, at the very least, that once the prelude begins, all conversation in the sanctuary ends. It means that maintaining silence is not some old-fashioned notion of propriety, cramping the style of a "friendly" congregation, nor is it the relic of cranky preachers who don't love crying babies enough to put up with them. In fact, it is a sacred obligation for those who wish to be still so that they can know God. There is a time to whisper and a time to shout. There is also a time to say nothing at all.

Quakers shouldn't have cornered the market on silence. It should be the essential partner in all our communication, and there should be moments in worship when we can just be *quiet* together for a moment, in prayer, after the reading of the text, after the sermon—especially after the sermon. A "moment of silent consideration" follows the sermon at the service in my parish. The idea is that the sermon is completed in the listener and that good things take time. Besides, when someone preaches to me in a powerful way, the last thing I want is for someone to jump up three seconds later and tack on the coda: "Wasn't what Rev. Jones shared with us today wonderful! I don't know about you, but I'm ready to put it to the test." That's when we would need the old grappling hook to appear from offstage and remove this intruder who has confused worship with a game show. What could be worse than hearing a cheerful "sound bite" summing up a sermon that only moments ago had us all standing at the edge of the Grand Canyon?

Music

Sometimes I think that preachers and ministers of music fight all the time because they are each jealous of the other's power. The word of God comes in many forms, but the combination of word and song is as old as revelation itself. The church was born singing and has never stopped. While the shape and substance of music is as varied as tongues and races, one thing is certain: We all want (and need) to step into that swiftly moving current. Like a boat pushing away from the shore and leaving the normal friction of the world behind, we love to float on a musical score, carried along by something as deep and wide as memory and hope. There's a reason we sing our way into and out of the sanctuary. And there's a reason, on Sunday afternoons, so many of us are still humming the hymns.

Music is such an important component of worship that it cannot help but either muffle or amplify the voice of the preacher. Hymns that are fundamentally out of step with the sermon are often a painful reminder to everyone in the sanctuary that someone isn't paying attention. It's not that every hymn needs to fit perfectly, but at least the one *following* the sermon should! In most churches, there are at least three hymns sung—a processional hymn, which is necessarily upbeat and grand; a preparatory hymn, which usually comes before the sermon and is more reflective or meditative; and a recessional hymn, which can often "complete" the sermon musically and provide a powerful form of musical "punctuation." On the other hand, the wrong hymn after the sermon makes those who plan worship seem sloppy, if not inconsiderate.

I firmly believe in allowing ministers of music to have as much freedom as possible when it comes to the selection of hymns and other worship music. Preachers do not respond well to being told what to preach, and the same is true of those who provide sacred music for us. Just the same, autonomy is not to be confused with lack of communication. Most ministers of music are more than happy to know ahead of time how they might better tailor the service to the message of the sermon. More often than not they truly regret missing the opportunity and will often express their regret after the service. "If I had known what the sermon was about, the choir could have sung 'such and such.'" By then, of course, it's too late.

At the time of this writing, I am keenly aware of the homiletical advantage of hymns that are in synch with sermons. Preaching from a recent lectionary passage (Lk. 15:1–10) on the parables of the lost sheep and the lost coin, I mentioned in the sermon that marvelous hymn, "There Is a Wideness in God's Mercy." Because my minister of music also follows the lectionary in his selection of hymns, we all went out singing that very hymn! The earlier reference to it in the sermon amplified our singing of the hymn. The hymn that had come before it, "God of the Sparrow, God of the Whale," had cleared my throat just before the sermon—preparing me to speak about a God whose math is remedial and whose nature is to tear apart the house until She finds us.

Anyone who has been in the ministry for even a short time knows that some of the nastiest church fights are over music. Yet it can be said more truthfully about few things: *You can't please all of the people all of the time.* Having said this, and counseling caution to any minister who would throw too much weight around when it comes to church music, my best advice is to pay attention to both congregational and denominational traditions. Melodies are truly "transconscious" elements of worship, and hymn lyrics are never changed easily for the same reason. What's more, music is one of those emotional "anchors" that can buy the preacher a little time when it comes to being "not so traditional" in the pulpit. Fred Craddock said it well:

> The liturgical setting is also vital for the freedom of preaching...and because the liturgy is not full of surprises, novelties, and gimmicks, the sermon is set free by this order to be unsettling and disorienting, as conditions and the gospel warrant. The liturgy and the sermon give the twin provisions, order and variation...Replace the structure with disorientation and the sermon which was intended to be disorienting is wasted in the turbulence, the participants having been overwhelmed rather than confronted. It is the altar which makes possible preaching and listening.[12]

The Lectionary

Of all the changes that I have made in my ministry over the last twenty years, none has brought more unexpected power, coherence, and unity than my decision to become a lectionary preacher. I've heard all the arguments for and against it, but I send you this word from out of the *parish:* The discipline of preaching a text you might not have chosen on your own, but that provides thematic and seasonal balance in the church year, makes the essential partnership between worship and preaching possible and practical as well. Not only is it unreasonable (if not arrogant) to assume that the preacher will know what text to choose week after week, but to avoid the struggle that is inevitable when preaching from that which the church has chosen, rather than what we have chosen, is to miss the opportunity to do more than put one's fingers on one's pulse and call it theology.

Again, the practical benefits are obvious. Hymns based on the lectionary are chosen without the preacher's constant need to make suggestions. The three-year calendar makes it possible to plan sermons, and worship services that complement them, months in advance. Liturgical elements can reflect the themes as well, and the entire worship service can have a coherent "refrain." To know that the great themes of the faith as well as the great texts of the church will circle around helps both preacher and hearer. To know that the pulpit is a place to faithfully serve those ideas that were around before the preacher arrived and that will still be around after the preacher

---

[12]Fred Craddock, *Preaching* (Nashville: Abingdon Press, 1985), 42–43.

is gone creates a servant model benefiting everyone involved. As a preacher who has been involved in more than my share of risky sermons, I can tell you that the text not only gives me permission to preach in the first place, but is the only safety I will ever know or deserve.

I agree with Paul Scott Wilson that only one text should be chosen, with the gospel text being the norm. Listeners are not coming to church hungry to know how the Old Testament, New Testament, epistle, and psalm selections relate to one another. They are hoping to know God. What does matter is that each text is read, and one is chosen through either an initial passion or an initial annoyance. "Texts that initially disturb us can produce excellent preaching."[13]

One of the most unexpected benefits of lectionary preaching and lectionary worship services is the idea that so many other worshiping communities are taking up the same themes on the same day. Instead of a "voice crying in the wilderness," we become part of a vast chorus ringing out across the ecclesiastical landscape. The liturgies and the messages will be as varied as the communities and their respective theologies, but more often than not there is a kind of collective energy that arises out of our collective endeavor. And consider this: If your Sunday school teachers use a lectionary-based curriculum, children will be giving their take on the text in the car on the way home. In my congregation this has sparked more than a few rich discussions with parents who wrestled with the same text in the sanctuary.

As a discipline, lectionary preaching and lectionary worship create an experience in which the text is at the center of Sunday morning. It is not a straightjacket, robbing the preacher of her freedom. When the train hits the school bus, or the tornado levels the elementary school, as Craddock has said, there is no need to feel obligated to preach about demon-possessed pigs. In my own experience, the topical sermon still has real power when it is done well according to guidelines like those set out by Ron Allen.[14] Besides, more often than you can imagine, the lectionary text speaks *powerfully* to world events, even to local tragedies, so much so that you'd swear the gospel was its own best argument–the answer to the problems of human

---

[13]Paul Scott Wilson, *The Practice of Preaching* (Nashville: Abingdon Press, 1995), 129–30.

[14]Ronald J. Allen, *Preaching the Topical Sermon* (Louisville, Ky.: Westminster/John Knox Press, 1992), 38–71.

existence. When the federal building was bombed in the city where I live and work, the lectionary text for the following Sunday was John's account of the disciples "hiding out for fear of the world." Thomas was in no mood to believe anything. In the wounded side of our city the body of Christ bled on to the street and then rose up. The sermon almost wrote itself.

In closing, I would say to the preacher: *Don't be jealous of all the ways that God can speak to people.* Do what you do as well as you can, and then don't forget that it isn't all that's being done! Consider the worship service to be as essential to the preparation and amplification of your voice as it is to the "tuning up" of all those beloved ears that sit before you. Preaching is not a solo performance; it is a sacred refrain from out of the depths of a "cloud of witnesses." It is worship that amplifies your voice. Standing on a mountain of prayer and song, you can see the promised land. Now tell us what you see and how it feels.

4

PREACHING AND THE SACRAMENT OF HOLY COMMUNION

Paul Scott Wilson

I welcome the opportunity to reconsider the relationship between the preached Word and the sacrament of holy communion. Accidents of history are largely responsible for my own denomination's[1] frequent celebration of holy communion, in spite of strong theological affirmations of frequent celebration in our theological heritage. Calvin's Geneva council rejected his insistence on weekly celebration in favor of quarterly; and although the Wesleys instituted a "eucharistic revival" and published a collection of 166 eucharistic hymns for their Methodist revivals,[2] the absence of sufficient ordained ministers riding their circuits dictated infrequent celebration. Prosper of Aquitaine's ancient dictum, *legem credendi lex statuat supplicandi* (the rule of praying establishes the rule of believing), still apparently holds true, for my own spirituality rests primarily in the word. As someone reared in a church with minimal ritual and that made a practice in those days of removing children for nearly all celebrations of communion, I use this opportunity to explore from the perspective of preaching what may be missing in simple services of the Word. How is the Word affected by its proximity to, or distance from, the table?

---

[1]The United Church of Canada originated in 1925 with a union of two-thirds of the Presbyterians, all the Methodists, and all the Congregationalists. *Holy communion* and the *Lord's supper,* are still the most common terms in our denomination, although those influenced by the liturgical movement favor *eucharist.* In this chapter, there is not space to also consider baptism. For convenience, I generally use the word *sacrament* here to refer to holy communion.

[2]Laurence Hull Stookey, *Eucharist: Christ's Feast with the Church* (Nashville: Abingdon Press, 1993), 87–88.

43

How are the prayers at the table to be distinguished from proclamation? Does their presence or absence affect the nature of what is preached?

Scriptural Background

In most New Testament texts dealing with preaching, there is no connection to the Lord's supper. No absolute distinction can be made among various words for preaching–commonly *angello, evangelizo, didasko, katangello, kerysso*–concerning form or content. Jesus authorizes preaching in the sending forth of the Twelve to proclaim the kingdom of heaven (Mt. 10:7; Lk. 9:2) and of the seventy-two for the same purpose (Lk. 10:1, 9). The Word they take with them is his Word: "What I say to you in the dark, tell in the light; and what you hear whispered, proclaim from the housetops" (Mt. 10:27). He accompanies them in the preaching in a manner understood in popular legal maxims of the day: "Whoever listens to you listens to me, and whoever rejects you rejects me, and whoever rejects me rejects the one who sent me" (Lk. 10:16). Moreover, the resurrected Christ commissions the disciples to baptize and preach (Mt. 28:19–20; Mk. 16:15–16; Acts 10:42) and sends the Holy Spirit upon them (Lk. 24:29; Jn. 20:22), promising to be with them always (Mt. 28:20).

Paul similarly speaks of preachers as those who are sent ("And how are they to proclaim him unless they are sent?" [Rom. 10:15]) and of the power of the message being a spoken and heard word through Christ ("So faith comes from what is heard, and what is heard comes through the word of Christ" [Rom. 10:17]). While in Matthew 10 and Luke 10, preaching is to be accompanied with healings, and in Paul with demonstrations of the Spirit and of power (1 Cor. 2:4), preaching in itself is an auditory event in which the Holy Spirit is active. "We speak of these things in words not taught by human wisdom but taught by the Spirit, interpreting spiritual things to those who are spiritual" (1 Cor. 2:13). Listeners who choose not to receive the message manifest their own unspiritual condition (1 Cor. 2:14). Paul did not question the authorization to preach, provided that the preachers preached Jesus Christ (Phil. 1:15–18), yet by the time of the epistle to Titus, preaching is the institutionalized responsibility of the bishop (Titus 1:5–9).

Although preaching in the New Testament does not normally imply the Lord's supper, many New Testament texts have eucharistic overtones and direct references to the Lord's supper and at times hint at links to preaching. Yet, as Geoffrey Wainwright says of worship practice in the apostolic age, the evidence is either fragmentary, indirect, or has to be interpreted in the light of later practice.[3]

Evidence falls into several categories:

(1) The synoptic narratives of institution (Mt. 26:26–29; Mk. 14: 22–25; Lk. 22:15–20) establish two important preaching emphases: First, the visual symbols of bread and wine point to the atoning sacrifice of Christ on the cross begun in the incarnation and completed in Jesus' death and the new covenant. They are what Augustine called *visible words* that witness to the identity and work of Jesus. Second, the narratives focus on the future, with resurrection and eschatological overtones ("I will never again drink of this fruit of the vine until that day when I drink it new with you in my Father's kingdom" [Mt. 26:29]). As such, the entirety of God's salvation purpose is attested.

(2) The feeding of the five thousand links feeding with preaching. Apart from the resurrection, this is the only miracle recorded in all four gospels. In the synoptics the feeding has eucharistic overtones, *flows from* the teaching of Jesus, and is a communal act of humility, sharing, love, and service, all inseparable from mission. In John 6, the feeding *leads to* Jesus' preaching to the crowd on the bread of life and his identification of himself as that bread and the future promise.

(3) The Emmaus appearance (Lk. 24:13–35) carries the suggestion of knowing Christ in two ways, in Word and sacrament.[4] Jesus' teaching along the road acts as a seal on the teachings they have received ("Were not our hearts burning within us...while he was opening the scriptures to us?" [Lk. 24:32]). His identity is made known to the disciples in the breaking of the bread.

(4) The breaking of bread that Jesus instructed is itself preaching *(katangello)* in 1 Corinthians 11:26 ("For as often as you eat this bread and drink the cup, you *proclaim* the Lord's death until he comes"). Markus Barth explains: "For Paul the death of Christ was and is good news, and to speak of

[3]Geoffrey Wainwright, "General Introduction," in Chelsea Jones, Geoffrey Wainwright, and Edward Yarnold, S.J., eds., *The Study of Liturgy* (New York: Oxford University Press, 1978), 34.

[4]I am indebted on this and other points to a conversation with Professor Stephen Farris of Knox College, Toronto.

Christ crucified is, according to him, the only proper way to speak of the Lord, for all the wisdom of God and the sum of the gospel are enclosed in him (1 Cor. 1:18–2:16). 'Proclaim the Lord's death'–during the Lord's supper means that at this table are to be expressed the pleasure and the joy that are caused by the crucifixion."[5] This proclamation and celebration has a social justice component: Food from the common meal is to be shared and the poor are to be treated equally, not excluded (1 Cor. 11:20–22).

The Early Church

These various scriptural emphases were shaped by the earliest Christian worship practices and, in turn, influenced the later church's worship practices. Tertullian, in speaking of baptism, translated *mysterion* as *sacramentum,* a Roman term for a public pledge (often military) that had sacred implications. In the East, *mysterion* did not come to have the restricted meaning of sacrament. In Paul, *mystery* refers to the core of the gospel and not specifically to the Lord's supper. Evidence is mixed concerning Paul's Corinthian community: (a) whether the assembly was weekly and (b) when assembled, whether there was one assembly with two phases or two types of gathering, one for the supper and the other for instruction and charisms.[6] Christians brought from the synagogue a service of the Word that consisted of readings from the law and the prophets, a sermon, and prayers. Paul's instructions imply that the wealthy Corinthians are proceeding to eat before the poor arrive after work and may suggest a gathering for the meal separate from worship. There are similarities in Luke, who says that the baptized devoted themselves to the apostles' teaching and fellowship, the breaking of bread, and the prayers (Acts 2:42), and spent much time together in the temple. They broke bread at home and ate their food with glad and generous hearts (2:46). They gathered on the first day of the week "to break bread" and Paul "continued speaking until midnight" (20:7). Peter G. Cobb claims that, from the earliest descriptions of the eucharist, it is clear that it could be divided in two parts, either of which might on

---

[5]Markus Barth, *Rediscovering the Lord's Supper: Communion with Israel, with Christ, and among the Guests* (Atlanta: John Knox Press, 1988), 45.

[6]C. P. M. Jones, "The New Testament," in Chelsea Jones, Geoffrey Wainwright, and Edward Yarnold, S.J., ed., *The Study of Liturgy* (New York: Oxford University Press, 1978), 155. Jones argues that the Corinthians "followed the meal with an extended instruction session" (p. 169).

occasion be held independently or in a different church building from the other.[7] These two parts Tertullian called the ministry of the Word and the offering of the sacrifice,[8] the seventh-century Byzantine church called the liturgy of the catechumens and the liturgy of the faithful,[9] the eleventh-century Western church likewise called the mass of the catechumens and the mass of the faithful,[10] and the church in Luther's and Calvin's day called the fore-mass and the mass, or the ante-communion and the communion service.

The prayer of thanksgiving that followed the meal—if indeed the Jewish tradition of the *birkat ha-mazon* was the model and origin of the great thanksgiving prayer—may, in fact, have functioned as a form of proclamation.[11] Laurence Hull Stookey argues that *anamnesis* ("Do this as often as you drink it in remembrance of me") was for Paul and the ancient Jews and Christians a participatory event, not a cerebral one.[12] In any case, *The First Apology of Justin Martyr*, around 150 C.E., records a union of Word and Lord's supper in a weekly pattern: Worship consisted of readings from the memoirs of the apostles or the writings of the prophets, preaching and prayers led by the president, presentation of the bread and wine, prayers and thanksgiving, a collective Amen, distribution of the elements, and collection and distribution of the benevolent offering.[13] Common practice, when the service of the Word was followed by service of the Lord's supper,

---

[7]Peter G. Cobb, "The Liturgy of the Word in the Early Church," in Chelsea Jones, Geoffrey Wainwright, and Edward Yarnold, S.J., eds., *The Study of Liturgy* (New York: Oxford University Press, 1978), 181.

[8]Ibid., 182.

[9]Hugh Wybrew, "The Byzantine Liturgy from the *Apostolic Confessions* to the Present Day," in Chelsea Jones, Geoffrey Wainwright, and Edward Yarnold, S.J., eds., *The Study of Liturgy* (New York: Oxford University Press, 1978), 210–11.

[10]Cobb, "Liturgy of the Word," 182.

[11]C. P. M. Jones concludes that the blessing and the distribution of the body of Christ before the common meal and of the blood of Christ after the meal was followed by an explanation: "It needs a *verbal* proclamation, for which there is no satisfactory place in Jewish tradition other than the extended thanksgiving after the meal" ("The New Testament," 33).

[12]It was "a corporate event in which the event remembered was experienced anew through ritual repetition" (Stookey, *Eucharist*, 30). In other words, in the taking, giving thanks, breaking, and distributing of the bread and cup, the congregation participated anew in the presence of the living Christ. From the beginning, it was not a cerebral and passive act of remembrance, in the manner that preaching could have been interpreted.

[13]Justin Martyr, "The First Apology of Justin Martyr," in Bard Thompson, ed., *Liturgies of the Western Church* (Philadelphia: Fortress Press, 1961), 8–9.

was that the catechumens were dismissed prior to communion and the doors of the church were locked,[14] a practice eventually ended in the Roman rite and continuing to the present in the East.[15]

Many of our questions about preaching and the Lord's supper cannot be answered conclusively. For instance, why did the prayers that evolved around the narrative of institution develop as they did? Why did preaching not take the burden of responsibility for interpreting the meaning of the Lord's supper? More speculatively, if the sacrament of the Lord's supper was practiced separate from proclamation of the Word, was the great prayer perceived to remove the need for preaching? The *Didache,* at the end of the first or early second century, already prescribes a method for giving thanks at eucharist that moves from reciting God's saving actions in the past to the future.[16] The messages that developed through the eucharistic prayers both shaped the understanding of the sacrament and rendered in words the heart of the gospel message as appropriate for preaching. Yngve Brilioth identified five key and complementary New Testament images that have dominated understandings of the eucharist at different times in the church's history: joyful thanksgiving, remembrance, community, sacrifice, and Christ's presence. To these James White adds two more: action of the Holy Spirit and foretaste of the final consummation of things.[17]

The Legacy of the Reformation

Throughout the history of the church, various reasons have been given for linking Word and table. Karl Barth said there were three forms of the Word of God (Jesus Christ himself, scripture, and proclamation). When asked about the sacraments, he responded, "Sacrament is included in the preached Word."[18] Augustine perceived Word and sacrament as forming a unity. He defined sacrament as a visible sign of an invisible grace or visible words–actions to which the Word comes with the same message as the sermon: "Let the Word be added to the element and it will become a sacrament."[19] The efficacy of the

---

[14]Wybrew, "Byzantine Liturgy," 211.

[15]Cobb, "Liturgy of the Word," 188.

[16]*Didache,* in *Early Christian Fathers,* ed. Cyril Richardson (Philadelphia: Westminster Press, 1953), 175.

[17]James F. White, *Sacraments as God's Self Giving: Sacramental Practice and Faith* (Nashville: Abingdon Press, 1983), 53–61.

[18]Karl Barth, *Karl Barth's Table Talk,* ed. John D. Godsey (Richmond, Va.: John Knox Press, 1963), 36.

[19]Augustine, *John's Gospel,* lxxx.3; cited by Calvin, *Institutes of the Christian Religion,* ed. John T. McNeill, Library of Christian Classics 20 and 21 (Philadelphia: Westminster Press, 1960), IV, 14, 4.

sacrament is expressed for him in practical ways in the individual's life. For example, concerning John 6:56 (Those who eat my flesh and drink my blood abide in me, and I in them) he said, the sign that one has eaten and drunk is this: if he remains and is abided, if he dwells and is indwelt, if he adhere in order that he not be forsaken.[20]

Luther said that "the chief and greatest aim of any Service is to preach and teach God's Word."[21] He also said, "the Lord neither required this Supper as necessary or established it by law, but left it free to everyone, saying, As often as you do this, etc."[22] He identified a range of reasons for regular and frequent linking of Word and table:

(1) This linking is fundamentally practical, he said, drawing on Augustine's notion of the visual: "It is true, such faith [from proclamation] is enough and truly accomplishes everything. But how could you think of this faith, sacrifice, sacrament, and testament if it were not visibly administered?"[23]

(2) Preaching is to be simple exposition of scripture and is closely linked to this sacrament: "For the preaching ought to be nothing but an explanation of the words of Christ, when he instituted the mass and said, 'This is my body, this is my blood,... etc.' What is the whole gospel but an explanation of this testament?" (*LW*, 35, 106)

(3) The sacrament also was a means of proclamation to those who would not be able to comprehend the sermon: "So every Christian, no matter how crude he may be, may be able to comprehend here in the sacrament the whole Christian doctrine, what he is to believe and what he is to do in faith" (*LW*, 36, 352), by which Luther meant to receive forgiveness, be saved, and be redeemed from death and hell.

---

[20]Augustine, *Commentary on the Fourth Gospel,* 26:18, quoted by Edward J. Kilmartin, S.J., "The Eucharistic Gift: Augustine of Hippo's Tractate 27 on John 6:60–70," in Chelsea Jones, Geoffrey Wainwright, and Edward Yarnold, S.J., ed., *The Study of Liturgy* (New York: Oxford University Press, 1978), 162.

[21]Martin Luther, "Preface, The German Mass and Order of Service, 1526," in Bard Thompson, ed., *Liturgies of the Western Church* (Philadelphia: Fortress Press, 1961), 129.

[22]Martin Luther, "Formula of Mass and Communion for the Church at Wittenberg, 1523," in Bard Thompson, ed., *Liturgies of the Western Church* (Philadelphia: Fortress Press, 1961), 117.

[23]Martin Luther, *Luther's Works,* gen. ed. Jaroslav Pelikan and Helmut T. Lehman, vol. 35 (Philadelphia: Muhlenberg Press, 1960), 104. Subsequent references to this series will be in-text, using the abbreviation *LW*.

(4) Preaching did something the sacrament did not do (at least as it had been practiced in the Roman Church)—it touched people's hearts: "Then the word brings Christ to the folk and makes him known in their hearts, a thing they never understood from the sacrament."[24]

(5) This sacrament elicits commitment to the proclaimed Word and to the community: "When you have partaken of this sacrament, therefore, or desire to partake of it, you must in turn share the misfortunes of the fellowship...As love and support are given you, you in turn must render love and support to Christ in his needy ones" (*LW,* 35, 54). "There are those, indeed, who would gladly share in the profits but not in the costs....they are unwilling in their turn to belong also to this fellowship. They will not help the poor, put up with sinners, care for the sorrowing, suffer with the suffering, intercede for others, defend the truth, and at the risk of [their own] life, property, and honor seek the betterment of the church and of all Christians" (*LW,* 35, 57).

(6) The efficacy of the sacrament relates to the neediness of the individual for the Word: "This sacrament is of little or no benefit to those who have no misfortune or anxiety, or who do not sense their adversity. For it is given only to those who need strength and comfort, who have timid hearts and terrified consciences, and who are assailed by sin or have fallen into sin" (*LW,* 35, 55). Finally, of course, the efficacy rested in faith: "Should Christ institute so great a thing in vain, without any use or profit?" (*LW,* 36, 352)

For Calvin, the marks of the church are the word of God purely preached and heard, and the sacraments administered according to Christ's institution.[25] Preaching without "the seal of the sacrament" nonetheless "can stand unimpaired" (*ICR,* IV, 14, 14). He suggested several reasons for them to be linked:

(1) The simplest reason for the sacrament was practical: "It is not so much needed to confirm [God's] sacred word as to

---

[24]Martin Luther, as quoted by Karl Barth, *The Doctrine of the Word of God,* trans. G. T. Thomson (New York: Charles Scribner's Sons, 1936), 78.

[25]John Calvin, *Institutes of the Christian Religion,* ed. John T. McNeill, Library of Christian Classics 20 and 21 (Philadelphia: Westminster Press, 1960), IV, 1, 9. Subsequent references to this work will be in text, using the abbreviation *ICR.*

establish us in faith in it" (*ICR*, IV, 14, 3). "By the elements of bread and wine, God condescends to lead us to himself, and to set before us in the flesh a mirror of spiritual blessings" (*ICR*, IV, 14, 3). While they add nothing new to the Word and are not to be confused with justification, the sacraments bring the clearest promises and represent them for us as painted in a picture from life (*ICR*, IV, 14, 5).

(2) Word and sacrament are part of the same office of the word of God (*ICR*, IV, 14, 17) and confirm each other (*ICR*, IV, 14, 5) by the action of the Holy Spirit who illumines our minds (*ICR*, IV, 14, 8–9). Preaching must make us understand what the visible sign means (*ICR*, IV, 14, 4); Christ is the matter or (if you prefer) the substance of all the sacraments, because in him they have all their firmness, and they do not promise anything apart from him (*ICR*, IV, 14, 16).

(3) Preaching was necessary for God to be known spiritually. In the same manner, a sacrament functions in relation to its receiver as a metaphor communicating spiritual truth: You must apprehend in faith the Word that is included there. As much, then, as you will profit through the sacraments in the partaking of Christ, so much profit will you receive from them (*ICR*, IV, 14, 15). Both preaching and the sacraments fail without the Holy Spirit.

(4) The sacrament functions also as a seal (Rom. 4:11) to this knowledge in preaching: "It is an outward sign by which the Lord seals on our consciences the promises of his good will toward us in order to sustain the weakness of our faith" (*ICR*, IV, 14, 1). Calvin uses other metaphors, variously calling the sacraments Augustine's visible Word, a picture, a pillar of faith, a mirror in which we contemplate the riches of God's grace (*ICR*, IV, 14, 5), and a guarantee (*ICR*, IV, 14, 12). So committed were Calvin's followers to the sacrament as a seal that some picked up the early church practice of locking the doors of the church following the sermon, not to prevent people from leaving, but to prevent those who had not heard the sermon from partaking of the sacrament.[26]

---

[26]See Bard Thompson, "John Knox," in Bard Thompson, ed., *Liturgies of the Western Church* (Philadelphia: Fortress Press, 1961), 292.

Calvin seems to make no distinction between preaching and the words of the great prayer following the narrative of institution, words that recite the promises that were left to us in it (*ICR,* IV, 17, 43). Since Word and sacraments share one office, both are proclamation, though the latter cannot stand separate from the former. He called the eucharistic prayers "living preaching": "Here [at the table] we should not imagine some magic incantation, supposing it enough to have mumbled the words, as if they were to be heard by the elements; but let us understand that these words are living preaching, which edifies its hearers, penetrates into their very minds, impresses itself upon their hearts and settles there, and reveals its effectiveness in the fulfillment of what it promises" (*ICR,* IV, 17, 39). This conformity of preaching and sacrament is in contrast to Zwingli (and many evangelical churches today), who understood communion, four times a year, as a bare memorial and not a means of grace.[27]

Both Luther and Calvin retained much of the Roman shape of the eucharistic prayers in their liturgies and hence their effect as relatively complete explications of the faith. Luther objected to the Roman canon of the mass—the order of service, prayers, and readings around the sacramental rites—on a number of scores, including the suppression of the Word, the offertory and its notion of a repeatable sacrifice (i.e., the denial of Christ's once-for-all sacrifice), and the practice of the words being addressed to the elements and not to the people.[28] He revised the canon in the Latin *Formula Missae,* which retained most of the Roman prayers. He also published an alternate and much simplified vernacular German mass in which, following the sermon and the creed, the preface was replaced by a substantial "public paraphrase of the Lord's Prayer" that served as a thanksgiving and explication of the faith. This was followed by an exhortation and invitation that led directly to the words of institution, consecration, and distribution.

Calvin followed the sermon with extensive general prayers that themselves explicated the faith in considerable detail, the words of

---

[27]After the words of institution in his liturgy, he imposed complete silence, except in the 1535 edition of the liturgy, when the reading of John, beginning with the Last Supper in John 13, was prescribed. See Bard Thompson, "Ulrich Zwingli: The Zürich Liturgy, 1525," in Bard Thompson, ed., *Liturgies of the Western Church* (Philadelphia: Fortress Press, 1961), 8–9.

[28]These prayers in the medieval church were often inaudible or mumbled, since several priests at many different altars might be reciting private masses. For a detailed discussion of Luther's revisions, see Bard Thompson, "Martin Luther," in Bard Thompson, ed., *Liturgies of the Western Church* (Philadelphia: Fortress Press, 1961), 95–105, especially 100–101.

institution, an expounding of the promises of Christ, excommunication of those who were obdurate sinners, and instruction concerning worthy participation. Thus, even the revised liturgies of Luther and Calvin preserved many of the functions, if not the forms, of the earlier prayers. *The Book of Common Prayer* of the Church of England simply revised the canon, in particular removing the emphasis on individual sacrifice.

Contemporary Reflection

Liturgies before and after the Reformation show close parallels between preaching in its various forms and expressions and the words and prayers of the sacrament. These prayers typically include various scriptural quotations, exhortations, invitations, remembrances, explanations, interpretations, and even "applications."[29] As Karl Barth says, for the reformers there are two kinds of proclamation, one "the ground of the promise laid down once for all" and the other "proclamation in the form of symbolic action."[30] Luther had spoken of Jesus as the one sacrament of the church–"The Holy Scriptures contain one sacrament only which is the Lord Jesus Christ himself."[31] This may have influenced Lutheran theologian Johannes Rupprecht in 1925 to claim that, "the Word is the audible sacrament and the sacrament is the visible Word."[32] Since the sermon develops the promises of the gospel upon which the sacraments are founded, it could conceivably take the place of some of the prayers. With all the Reformation and counter-Reformation upheaval, it seems surprising that no interest was shown in combining more closely the sermon and the sacramental rite, or in greater clarification of their differences.

Still, we have some clues from the reformers concerning these matters that influence contemporary worship and homiletical practices. The practice of reading prepared sermons in some churches

---

[29]For example, *The Westminster Confession* stipulates that after the words of institution, "the minister may, when he seeth requisite, explaine and apply," in Bard Thompson, ed., *Liturgies of the Western Church* (Philadelphia: Fortress Press, 1961), 369.

[30]Karl Barth, *The Doctrine of the Word of God,* trans. G. T. Thomson (New York: Charles Scribner's Sons, 1936), I, 1, 77.

[31]Martin Luther, as translated from the Weimar Edition of his works (vol. 6, 1888, 86), in Markus Barth, *Rediscovering the Lord's Supper* (Atlanta: John Knox Press, 1988), 101. Barth notes that the later Luther seems to forget his earlier understanding, and that it is picked up by Eberhard Jüngel in *Evangelische Theologie* 26 (1966): 334–36. See also Jn. 1:14; 2 Cor. 4:4; Col. 1:15; 2:9; and Heb. 1:3.

[32]As quoted by Karl Barth in *The Doctrine of the Word of God,* 79. Robert Jenson picks up the notion of the Word as "audible sacrament," without mention of a source, in his "The Sacraments," in *Christian Dogmatics,* ed. Robert W. Jenson, Hans Schwartz, and Paul Sponheim (Philadelphia: Fortress Press, 1984), 303.

could have contributed both to a perceived similarity of Word and sacraments (since both were read) as well as to their differences. Luther advocated the reading of published sermons, all or in part, "for the sake of the preachers who could not do any better, but also to prevent the rise of enthusiasts and sects."[33] The Church of England similarly resorted often to homilies that were read, largely because of a lack of capable priests.[34] Yet for many Protestants, preaching and extemporaneous prayer were to be in demonstration of the Spirit and of power. The admonitioners attacked Anglican homilies on the basis that reading is not feeding.[35] The Puritan Thomas Cartwright phrased the matter pointedly, "As the fire stirred giveth more heat, so the Word, as it were, blown by preaching, flameth more in the hearers than when it is read."[36] For the Puritans, not least, comparisons between preaching and the readings or recitations of orderly prayers for the sacrament would be misplaced.

Moreover, while considerable progress had been made in the medieval church to recover preaching, the Reformers made preaching their cornerstone based on the centrality of scripture and speaking and hearing as the means of faith. The spoken and published sermon became the primary vehicle to disseminate doctrinal positions and reforms. Lengthy sermons were the norm. Concern with efficiency and uniformity were not the issues of the day–the dominantly oral world of the time moved in a different direction, toward accumulation, clarification, and repetition.

Key differences between Word and sacrament have to do not with content, for each is a means of grace, but with the form of each and the manner of God's action in each to accomplish God's saving purposes. The words of the sermon function in a manner similar to the words surrounding the action of the sacrament: The sermon expounds the Word even as the prayer explains the sacrament. The prayer identifies the promises contained in the sacrament and creates, as it were, an intentional surplus rather than an economy of meaning. The sermon moves from a particular place or places in the broad biblical story to the concreteness of our hope in Christ. The

---

[33]Martin Luther, "Preface, The German Mass and Order of Service, 1526," in Bard Thompson, ed., *Liturgies of the Western Church* (Philadelphia: Fortress Press, 1961), 132. Luther also wrote his *Church Postil* for this purpose.

[34]Bard Thompson, "The Middleburg Liturgy of the English Puritans," in Bard Thompson, ed., *Liturgies of the Western Church* (Philadelphia: Fortress Press, 1961), 312–13, 318.

[35]Ibid., 318.

[36]Ibid.

prayers by common tradition move similarly from God's saving actions in history to the concreteness of Christ's self-giving at this table, in this bread and wine, which function metonymically as the one table throughout the world that is spread for all God's people.

To say that the sermon pronouces the fullness of the gospel message through the particularities of biblical texts could imply that every sermon should be narrowly christocentric, in the manner that the sacrament is largely and necessarily christocentric. However, to preach in such a manner would ironically result in something less than the fullness of the gospel being proclaimed. Fred Craddock calls preachers to preach what Paul and Mark called the "gospel of God" (Rom. 1:1; Mk. 1:14), respecting both the whole Bible as a means of God's self-revelation and the integrity of the Old Testament witnesses.[37] James F. White puts the matter this way as he considers the advantages of the lectionary for preaching accompanying the sacrament: Preachers "can now preach Moses and Jeremiah and Acts and Revelation, because the Eucharist always preaches Christ."[38] Still, we cannot preach apart from the lens that Jesus Christ provides in our reading of all scripture, nor separate from speaking of the three Persons of the Trinity (trinitarian speech is inherently christocentric), and our words might normally move, at least by the end of the sermon, in some way to the resurrection that is both the starting place and ending point of faith. Elizabeth Achtemeier's somewhat unwieldy suggestion that, in preaching, an Old Testament text should always be paired with a New Testament text is at least one means of giving practical expression to this conviction.[39] However, one does not need a specific New Testament text to be able to speak of the Christ event or to be able to identify how the meaning found in an Old Testament text resonates with the central narrative or symbols of the faith.

The sacrament is also an expression of the fullness of the gospel, although in a somewhat different sense. One of the reasons the words at the table are called, in some traditions, "the great prayer" is that they can be said to take the place of the other prayers of the church, or that the great prayer takes them into itself. When the prayer follows the model of Hippolytus of Rome, it typically includes some

---

[37]See Fred B. Craddock's discussion of this in "The Gospel of God," in *Preaching as a Theological Task: World, Gospel, Scripture*, ed. Thomas G. Long and Edward Farley (Louisville, Ky.: Westminster John Knox Press, 1996), 73–81.

[38]White, *Sacraments as God's Self Giving*, 64.

[39]Elizabeth Achtemeier, *The Old Testament and the Proclamation of the Gospel* (Philadelphia: Westminster Press, 1973), 142–44. See also her *Preaching from the Old Testament* (Louisville, Ky.: Westminster/John Knox Press, 1989), 56–59.

form of opening dialogue; praise and thanksgiving, reciting God's works (with the *Sanctus* and *Benedictus*); exhortation and invitation; confession; the narrative of institution; *anamnesis,* or remembrance, particularly of Christ's passion; resurrection, ascension, and future coming in glory; *epiclesis;* and trinitarian doxology. Normally it also includes the Lord's Prayer and a creed. These prayers and various adaptations of them by the Reformers represent not only an adequate explanation of what takes place in the sacrament, they represent in some ways the most complete compressed narrative and trinitarian expression of the center of the faith. Even as the sermon articulates a specific Word for this congregation today, the sacramental prayers articulate the specific nature of the faith of the church at large.

The words surrounding the sacrament are not only *prayer,* for they include words spoken to God, words spoken for God (e.g., "This is my body..."), and words spoken to one another in God's name,[40] as in the passing of the peace or the distribution of the elements. There has been debate in Lutheran circles as to whether the words of institution are themselves proclamation or prayer.[41] Still, the spoken words are predominantly prayer, and this too distinguishes them from the sermon. As prayer, the sacramental words are something humans offer to God, albeit with the help of the Holy Spirit and as a means of conversation with God—in this case, in preparation for the sacrament. Moreover, in most traditions prayer is "speech addressed to the first person of the Trinity, we speak through Christ, and by the power of the Holy Spirit. Christian prayer, ever since the early centuries, has been addressed to the first person through Jesus Christ."[42]

Preaching, by contrast, is heralding, announcing, or proclaiming and is addressed to the congregation. It is at least a human act. It is an offering the preacher makes on behalf of the congregation and for which the preacher is set apart in ordination. In this regard it parallels prayer. Gerhard O. Forde presents it as the final step in the movement from the primary discourse of God in the Bible, through the secondary discourse about God in systematic theology, to the primary discourse of God in the present.[43] It is a Word of hope, rendered

---

[40]White, *Sacraments as God's Self Giving,* 18.

[41]Arnold F. Krugler, "The Words of Institution: Proclamation or Prayer?" *Concordia Journal* 22 (March 1976): 53–60. He argues for the placement of the words of institution either before or after the eucharistic prayer, but that it should not be part of it lest the act be perceived as a transaction with God.

[42]White, *Sacraments as God's Self Giving,* 18.

[43]Gerhard O. Forde, *Theology Is for Proclamation,* Fortress Resources for Preaching (Minneapolis: Fortress Press, 1990), 4–6.

by the preacher specifically and uniquely for today, which convicts people of the futility of their own attempts to save themselves and liberates them through reliance on what has been accomplished for them on the cross.

Yet Protestant pneumatology affirms "that here, in this human and therefore entirely fallible act [of preaching], it may be that the eternal shall once more invade the temporal and human souls glimpse once more their true origin and destiny."[44] Preaching in this more significant sense is God's act, not a human act. A unity exists between preaching and scripture, which is one reason the word *sermon* in John Knox's *The Forme of Prayers* refers to both the scripture reading and the proclamation.[45] As Heinrich Bullinger said in the Second Helvetic Confession, "The Preaching of the Word of God is the Word of God."[46] For the Reformers, the sermon and its doctrines were the Bible in other words. Christ gives himself to the church as the Word, which is to be understood, believed, received in power, and acted on. The human dimension merely obscures the Word. Calvin said that the preacher "does not depart from Holy Scripture lest the pure word of God be obscured by the filth of men."[47] Luther and Barth also said that the preacher is to preach scripture and only scripture—although their sermons and Calvin's demonstrate that they in fact incorporated human experience in their preaching at every step. Nonetheless, focus on the human dimension can easily obscure the fact that preaching is ordained by God, that the preacher is a servant of the Word, and that preaching is God's action in speaking to the gathered community the words on which they need to feed for their upbuilding. Thus, to speak of Word and sacrament as Word and act is somewhat misleading, for both are acts, both in the human and, more importantly, in the divine perspective.[48] And to draw the parallel too closely between the sermon, which Christ preaches, and the prayers, which we offer and which prepare us for the sacrament, would also be a mistake.

---

[44]Douglas John Hall, *Confessing the Faith: Christian Theology in a North American Context* (Minneapolis: Fortress Press, 1996), 355.

[45]Thompson, "John Knox," 291.

[46]"The Second Helvetic Confession," in *The Constitution of the Presbyterian Church (U.S.A.): Part I, The Book of Confessions* (Louisville, Ky.: The Office of the General Assembly of the Presbyterian Church [U.S.A.], 1996), 55.

[47]John Calvin, "La Manière et Fasson," in Bard Thompson, ed., *Liturgies of the Western Church* (Philadelphia: Fortress Press, 1961), 216.

[48]Karl Barth argued that the primary emphasis be Word and faith, since the sacrament was a confirmation of the Word (Barth, *The Doctrine of the Word of God,* 79).

In some ways the sermon has closer parallels with the sacrament itself, that is, with the partaking of the elements in faith, rather than with the recitation of the prayers. Here Christ, who presides at the table, makes visible the giving of himself, broken even unto death, to his community and unites them, in all of their diversity, in his body for service to the world, something that was already evident in the preaching of the gospel. Both preaching and sacrament function as embodiments of the Word, as Charles Rice has argued notably.[49] In preaching, the Word takes shape, both in the course of preaching and throughout the week, in the lives of the people as they seek to live out the good news. The Word alone is adequate for faith. Paul Hoon cites concern for the fullness of the gospel as the reason for adding the sacrament:

> It was said of Luther that in any time of the church year in which he happened to be preaching, he proclaimed the fullness of the Word: "For him and his hearers, every day was Christmas and Good Friday and Easter and Pentecost." But we are not Luthers. And whereas preaching by itself does this occasionally, sacrament and sermon together do it almost inevitably.[50]

Hoon may limit too precisely to the actual words of the preacher what God is accomplishing through the sermon, and may lean too much in the direction of *ex opere operato* with his use of "inevitably," as though the performance of the work automatically ensures its desired effect, but his basic point is important. The inadequacy of our own words to express the mystery that we proclaim in Christ is most clearly compensated in the visual reenactment of our faith to which Christ joins himself. This action depends on words while at the same time it exhausts all words, its meaning and significance never being fully represented or enclosed by those words.

In this sacrament, Christ unites his presence with the bread and wine and visibly unites his life with our own, so that he may live in us and lead us to his purposes. In faith, believers participate in the reconciliation Christ offers with God and neighbor in ways that are also visible testimonies to his presence, for instance, in *koinonia* and in other "demonstrations of the Spirit and of power" that are the marks

---

[49]Charles Rice, *The Embodied Word: Preaching as Art and Liturgy,* Fortress Resources for Preaching (Minneapolis: Fortress Press, 1991). He argues for preaching in a sacramental context that will help the preacher to embody the Word and to avoid moralism, egotism, and other preaching errors.

[50]Paul Hoon, *The Integrity of Worship: Ecumenical and Pastoral Studies in Liturgical Theology* (Nashville: Abingdon Press, 1971), 147.

of the realm of God. We have seen that both Paul and Luther spoke of the fellowship that is shaped at Christ's table as being inclusive, without economic or other barriers; Calvin used the phrase, "He died for all…without discrimination."[51] In other words, what is made manifest by the Holy Spirit in and through the sacrament is what is best spoken about in the power of the Holy Spirit in the sermon—Christ drawing all humanity and creation to himself and God's eternal purpose. This movement takes form and shape in the self-giving and reconciling life of the community of faith.

Other Matters

There have been Christian groups, such as the Society of Friends, that deny all the outward forms of Christianity, including preaching and the sacraments, or, such as the Salvation Army, that have no sacraments. The Oxford Movement denied grace to preaching and confined it to the sacraments: "Sacraments, not preaching, are the sources of divine grace."[52] For the most part, however, historical discussions concerning Word and sacrament affirm the primacy of the Word, and contemporary discussions in Protestant contexts generally concern the frequency of holy communion. The unity of Word and sacrament may seem to be the issue, yet the office of Word and sacrament can be affirmed without insisting that all services of the Word be accompanied by the table. Such insistence was never the intention of the Reformers. Even if Calvin had been able to convince his council to have weekly communion in every congregation, or if Wesley had been able to field sufficient ordained ministers, the services through the week and on Sunday afternoons or evenings would have remained services of the Word. People have commonly argued that reverence for holy communion, rather than lack of reverence, determines infrequent celebration. One does not need to subscribe to this argument to affirm that practices of spirituality are important and change slowly, and then only with the consent and practice of the community. Evidence is still lacking that the current liturgical movement brings stronger faith.

Still, there are good reasons for weekly communion. James F. White thinks the two strongest reasons are: (1) Preaching is at its best accompanied by the eucharist, for preaching does not then need to carry the entire weight of the service and can more easily be based

---

[51]Calvin, "Manière et Fasson," 219.
[52]"Advertisement," in *Tracts for the Times,* vol. 1 (London: J. G. & F. Rivington; Oxford: J. H. Parker, 1854), iv.

anywhere in scripture[53]; and (2) from an anthropological perspective, humans need the sign-act of the eucharist because "humans express and perceive self-giving by seeing and hearing it made manifest."[54] Douglas John Hall argues creatively that Word and sacraments hold together the individual and collective conflicting tendencies in the church that are the result of an insufficient realization of the lordship of Jesus Christ. Thus, it is up to us "to attempt in whatever ways open to us to make more real and more concrete the presence of the One who will retain the legitimate headship of the body, wrestling it from *whichever faction* seeks to possess it, and causing the tensions that inhere in this relation to contribute to the *life* of the church, rather than to its death."[55]

Preaching currently has many critics. In every age it is popular to lament the state of preaching, and it is hard to evaluate the relative merits of such claims. Such claims are made because people sense that the church is less than it could be and recognize that preaching remains central to the health and well-being of congregational life. If change is to come, it will commonly need to include preaching. Hall is one of those in our age who holds the quality of preaching in low esteem. He complains of "a slow but effective ecclesial dry rot" that is preventing preaching from rising above the mundane.[56]

> If preaching today strives to be entertaining or "helpful" rather than edifying, convincing, and convicting, it is at least in part because so few preachers are themselves immersed in the theological and other disciplines that make for "wisdom"—a term that is too often associated with the kind of "spirituality" that is indifferent to learning...The fact is, "many whom the churches do not have," as well as a significant number of those whom they "have," are waiting to see whether anything approximating wisdom can come out of Nazareth![57]

Is weekly celebration of holy communion what is needed to bring preaching to a place of recovery? Such practice could add supportive breadth and depth to what is being offered in the sermon in a variety of ways. Yet, too often the call for frequent celebration, however appropriate it may be, sounds like a diminishment of preaching and all

[53]White, *Sacraments as God's Self Giving,* 64.
[54]Ibid., 65.
[55]Hall, *Confessing the Faith,* 113.
[56]Ibid., 350.
[57]Ibid., 351.

that it has been and can be in the Protestant tradition.[58] My own concern, in closing, is not to hasten the resolution of this tension, but to explore it further by returning to the opening question: What is lost when preaching is unaccompanied by holy communion?

In answering we may remember that the absence of the sacrament is not the absence of what is necessary for faith, nor is it the absence of all that is signified by the sacrament: The proclamatory function of the great prayer can still be embraced by what was called the pastoral prayer and is now often called the prayers of the people, which can follow the structure and content of the great prayer. We also need not assume that what is lost is all on the side of preaching, for the rich significance of the sacrament may also suffer from infrequent celebration, even as frequent celebration might lead to it's being taken for granted. Furthermore, from the Reformed and Methodist perspectives, something is also to be lamented when the art of extemporaneous prayer and the pastoral prayer is lost from the church, as is the case in many churches today, where it is sometimes replaced by printed prayers that are collectively read in monotone and often seem less than prayerful.[59]

Elsewhere I have identified two key problems with North American preaching. One is the absence of a focus on God and what God is doing.[60] Celebration of the sacrament should not and will not relieve preachers of addressing this problem in their sermons, but it can reinforce their attempts to cast people onto God's resources and not their own. If there is question about whose word is being heard in the sermon, the recitation of God's acts in history, combined with the visual impact of God's action in the sacrament, may impress upon members that Christ is in fact presiding in and over the church and at the table. God can appear more intimate and immediate when preaching is joined to the sacrament, for God is providing food for our daily needs in a common meal. Salvation can become less abstract when it is shaped by people gathered around a table partaking of the goodness of God and giving thanks.

---

[58]This sense is all the more acute because of the influence of Anglican Dom Gregory Dix's monumental study of the eucharist, *The Shape of the Liturgy* (London: Adam and Charles Black, 1945). He sums up his review of the Reformation with his claim, "The Protestant idea has never had in itself sufficient content to embrace either the whole essence of the Christian religion or the whole complexity of human life" (639).

[59]James F. White comments that preachers either have or do not have the gift for the pastoral prayer. White laments its use as instruction. Like so many scholars, he does little to ensure that it might be taught, nor does he recognize the instruction in the great prayer as an important model. See his *Introduction to Christian Worship,* rev. ed. (Nashville: Abingdon Press, 1990), 162–63.

[60]See my *The Four Pages of the Sermon* (Nashville: Abingdon Press, 1999).

A second problem in preaching is what I call "claustrophobia" induced by many contemporary pulpits. This problem is partly spatial: Preachers tend to be too centered on this congregation and these people, rarely bothering to seek God in the world beyond this church, city, county, country, or culture. The "Lord of my life" is proclaimed, but the "Lord of all" who is revealed in scripture is largely ignored. God is reduced to the size of individual knowledge and experience. When the sacrament accompanies preaching, by contrast, the visual sense of individuals putting aside their differences and becoming one is important, for the people gathered here, from different walks and stations of life, are now family. They represent the radical diversity of Christians around the world who are gathered around this one table, equally sharing this one meal, in one fellowship, with one ruler. This profound symbolism needs to be preached occasionally if it is to be found at the table, and because it is found at the table, it will influence the preaching of the church.

The problem of claustrophobia has temporal dimensions as well as spatial. Preaching gets too easily locked into our time, to the exclusion of the unique faith communities that have given us the biblical witness or that have handed us our traditions. Equally significant, and even more prone to exclusion, is a vision of the future, an understanding of the end times that puts the troubles of the moment into appropriate perspective under the sovereignty of Jesus Christ, who reigns over all time and space. Thus, what we taste in this moment, gathered around the table with the community of saints from all ages, is what God has in store for all creation through the power of the Holy Spirit. This is not pie in the sky but bread in the hand, the autocracy of the present moment concretely overthrown by a divine love that is poured out through all ages, one that knows no temporal boundaries or limitations. Without this strong eschatological flavor of the sacrament, preaching is more likely to get buried in the morass of daily struggles.[61] Preachers in such circumstances tend to look to the future with a magnifying glass, seeing only what is up close and only what they know well, when they need to use binoculars or a telescope. If we take the long view, what we will see will be far more liberating, just, inclusive, loving, and inspiring of faith than we had dared to hope.

---

[61]One of the best discussions of eschatology and the sacraments is Geoffrey Wainwright, *Eucharist and Eschatology* (New York: Seabury Press, 1981), especially 154. See also Marianne H. Micks, *The Future Present: The Phenomenon of Christian Worship* (New York: Seabury Press, 1970), 171–78.

5

THE CHRISTIAN YEAR AND THE REVISED COMMON LECTIONARY:

Helps and Hindrances to Worship Planners and Preachers

Shelley E. Cochran

Thirty years ago both the church year and the lectionary were largely unheard of in many long-established churches. With the exception of Episcopalians and Lutherans, many "mainline" congregations observed a year that consisted primarily of Easter, Christmas, and occasional special Sundays (Mother's Day, Rally Day, and some times Homecoming Day). For some congregations, there was no Lent or Advent, no great fifty days of Easter or Day of Pentecost, and certainly no Reign of Christ or Trinity Sunday.

Since the publication of the *Roman Lectionary for Mass,* however, the observance of the Christian year and the popularity of lectionaries, particularly among congregations in non-Catholic traditions, have increased dramatically. Now, thanks in part to liturgical renewal movements, traditions that earlier would have ignored holy days have now completely embraced them. Even Protestant churches that in the past actively resisted both the lectionary and the Christian year as too "Catholic" now hold Easter vigils and read virtually the same texts as their Roman counterparts across the street.

This shift brings with it both positive and negative consequences for Protestant worship planners and preachers. On the positive side of the ledger, the use of the lectionary ensures that a wide range of scripture will be read in worship. Observing the Christian year ensures that the faithful will be regularly reminded of the foundational stories of the church's faith. Both the lectionary and the year provide a tangible connection to the wisdom and practice of earlier generations of Christians. Both also provide a visible sign of ecumenical unity. Most important, both ensure that worship is appropriately focused on Christ and not on whatever might have captured the popular imagination at the moment.

On the other hand, both the use of the lectionary and the observance of the year on which it is based are not without problems. The lectionary, for example, is by nature an interpretive document. It does not include all the Bible, nor does it present the scriptures within their canonical context. The lectionary is also a human creation and thus reflects the interests of its compilers. It also reflects fallout from old theological controversies and assumptions from ancient theological understandings, some of which are no longer accepted or have since been discredited.

The Christian year, while it has many virtues, also has its problematic side. For instance, it uses an ancient hermeneutic that in some cases is no longer helpful. It has a strong historical focus. It also depends heavily on the gospel of Luke. (This is particularly noticeable in year B when readings from the gospel of Mark have to be supplemented with readings from Luke and John to fill out a church calendar that is completely foreign to it.)

In this chapter, I explore the Christian year, the Revised Common Lectionary, and their influence on worship and preaching. I begin by looking at the relationship of the Christian year to the lectionary. I examine the themes and theological interests reflected in both. I explore the structure of the lectionary and the year on which it is based, with particular attention to the way that structure shapes the way the Bible is interpreted in worship. Finally, I identify ways that worship planners and preachers can make informed choices in their use of the lectionary and their observance of the Christian year.

The Relationship between the Christian Year and the Lectionary

The first step toward understanding the way in which the Christian year and the lectionary influence preaching is to understand the way the two work together to exert that influence. The relationship between the year and the lectionary is dynamic and highly symbiotic. Indeed, the year and the lectionary are so closely connected that it is often difficult to determine which is the primary influence in any given instance. Such a close relationship is not surprising, however, for the year and the lectionary, in many respects, developed together. The year gives the lectionary its basic structure and theological themes, and the lectionary gives the year concrete expression in the readings assigned to each Sunday or feast day.

So, while the Christian year is the primary influence on preaching, the impact it has is mediated through the readings of the lectionary. Through those readings, the year influences which readings will be available for preaching and when those readings will be preached. It also influences the context in which those readings are preached (i.e., the liturgical season and links with other assigned readings). By encouraging the lectionary to include certain verses while excluding others according to the liturgical season, the Christian year even influences the length of the readings to be preached, albeit indirectly.

The Christian Year and the Lectionary as Editors of Scripture

Although several attempts have been made over the centuries, most notably in seventeenth-century Puritan New England, no schema for reading through the entire Bible in the context of public worship has ever taken hold. Three primary factors account for this. First, there is the nature of public worship itself. At its best, worship is dynamic and fluid. It invites participation on the part of the worshipers. It involves color, movement, and action. To be truly effective, worship must also include sacrament as well as Word, table as well as pulpit. As a result, public worship does not readily lend itself to long periods of reading, which would be required for the entire Bible to be covered in a reasonable length of time.

Second, the attention spans of most worshipers today do not lend themselves to long periods of public reading, either. Conditioned by the fast pace and frequent breaks characteristic of television, most worshipers today would not be capable of listening to long passages of scripture, nor would they likely be interested in doing so.

And third, the nature of the scriptures themselves does not invite reading through them verse by verse. As anyone who has tried to do so privately can attest, some parts of the Bible are more edifying than others. Between the beautiful poetry and gripping narratives, the Bible contains long, often interminable sections of statistics, genealogies, gruesome war stories, and diatribes against heretics. None of these invite public reading, either.

As a result, the Bible most Christians have heard in worship has, by necessity, always been abridged in some way, most often by the use of a lectionary. Before the scriptures even reach the pews, decisions about which passages and which verses in those passages will be included in worship have already been made. In some cases those decisions were made centuries ago, in other cases they were made within the last several years.

In the Revised Common Lectionary, decisions about which parts of scripture to include or omit were made primarily in four ways. Passages were chosen either because they were traditional, they fit the themes of the Christian year, they were doctrinally significant, or they were considered particularly edifying for the church. Individual verses within passages were often included or excluded for the same reasons. In practical terms, this means that a significant portion of the Bible never appears in worship. In many cases, this is appropriate. The long lists in Numbers, for example, and the war narratives in Joshua are rightly reserved for other times when they can be treated in a more thorough fashion than is possible in public worship.

In other cases, however, passages that deserve to be heard are not. Stories of biblical women are primary examples of this. Much of the story of Ruth, for instance, is missing from the lectionary. So is most of the story of Esther. Hagar and the Hebrew midwives did not appear in the lectionary until very recently.

Difficult and challenging portions of scripture are another example of passages that deserve to be heard and often are not. Reading about the political intrigue that surrounded the ascension of David to the throne, for example, might be instructive for congregations today. So might some of James's insights on classism or a few of Paul's accounts of conflicts in the early church. Exclusive use of the lectionary, however, denies such opportunities.

Other omitted passages that deserve to be heard include portions of scripture that offer unique viewpoints. Qoheleth's reflections in Ecclesiastes, for instance, might not be exactly edifying on the surface, but they certainly speak to the mood of many people today and could offer a bridge to reaching them. Jonah's backhand attack on religious and cultural exclusivism is also unfamiliar to most congregations, but ought not be. So is Mark's image of Jesus as the "strong man" doing battle with cosmic evil. These passages, too, do not get the attention they deserve in the lectionary.

At the same time, other passages of scripture, such as the prologue and passion narrative in John, are given special emphasis. These passages appear in the lectionary several times. Some appear every year, others appear two or even more times in one year. Certain portions of scripture are also emphasized. Isaiah 55–66, for instance, has more readings taken from it than any other portion of scripture. The psalms have their own special reading each Sunday, as do the gospels.

Decisions to omit, edit, or emphasize certain scriptures have an enormous impact on preaching, an impact that is often largely unnoticed. Such decisions influence the scope of scripture that is available for preaching. They influence the parameters of the passages chosen for preaching. They even influence how often a particular passage of scripture will be available for preaching and when. These decisions have an enormous impact on a congregation's understanding and knowledge of the scriptures. This is particularly true in North America today, where the only Bible most people encounter is the one they hear on Sunday morning. For such people, if a passage or particular portion of scripture never appears in the lectionary, chances are they will not hear it at all. If such passages are never read in worship or interpreted in a sermon, it is, in effect, as if they do not exist. In a similar way, if a particular passage or portion of scripture is repeated several times, it becomes familiar. It takes on special significance. It becomes, in essence, a canon within a canon.

This editing function is of particular concern for women and minorities. When stories of biblical women do not appear in the lectionary, their important witness is effectively silenced. Not only that, the present-day witness of women is often muted as well. Likewise, when the experience of people of color in the Bible (which is most of the experience recorded in the Bible) is not included in the lectionary, or worse, treated as if it were white experience, the whole church suffers. Fortunately, recent editions of the lectionary have taken strides to address this issue, but much work still remains.

The Christian Year and the Lectionary
as Biblical Interpreters

The lectionary and the Christian year not only edit the scriptures available for preaching, they also interpret them. Indeed, the power of the lectionary and the year to interpret scripture exerts a surprising degree of influence. It affects our understanding of scripture. It affects our interpretation of scripture. It affects our use of scripture in worship and preaching as well.

Passages are interpreted, for instance, by the way they are placed in the lectionary. Readings are also interpreted by the way they are associated with one another or with a particular season in the year. Passages are even interpreted by the way they are used in worship, that is, by whether they are read but not preached or whether they are read as a scripture lesson for the day or used in another part of the liturgy, perhaps as a prayer or call to worship.

This interpretive function is subtle and indirect. In most cases, neither the lectionary nor the church year tells us that we are being led in particular hermeneutical directions. Instead, most of this interpretation is done behind the scenes.

Because it is so subtle, the interpretive function of the lectionary and the year is largely subliminal in its effects. The particular view of scripture found in the lectionary and the year is so intricately woven into their fabrics that it seems almost self-evident. It is so deeply embedded, so well ingrained, that most hardly notice it, much less question it.

The lectionary and year interpret scriptures used in worship and preaching in three basic ways—through the structure of the year, the themes of the year, and the structure of the lectionary. The most important way the Christian year and the lectionary influence our use of scripture in worship is through the structure of the Christian year itself. This structure not only provides the lectionary the festivals and seasons that give it its characteristic shape, it also influences the selection and placement of scriptural passages available for preaching. Indeed, if there is one overriding influence on our understanding and interpretation of scripture in worship, it is this almost complete domination of calendar over canon.

The first and possibly most influential way that the structure of the Christian year interprets the scriptures used for preaching is through its use of an ancient hermeneutic. This hermeneutic was developed by the early church and arose out of two major concerns. The first was an effort to make sense of the death and resurrection of Jesus. The second was the early church's attempt to deal with the growing tension between itself and the synagogue. Both necessitated a new look at the scriptures of the early church's Hebrew faith.

The hermeneutic that developed out of these concerns was both a hermeneutic of proclamation designed to "prove" that Jesus of Nazareth was indeed the Messiah "according to the Scriptures," and a defensive hermeneutic designed to justify the followers of the "Way" before Jewish authorities. This ancient hermeneutic, which the church year subsequently inherited, employed several specific interpretive methodologies. It made heavy use of typology. It interpreted the Hebrew Scriptures from a prophecy/fulfillment mode. And it employed an eschatology that was primarily a realized eschatology.

To prove Jesus was the Messiah, for example, the early church searched the Hebrew Scriptures for types prefiguring Christ. Certain passages, such as Psalm 22 and Psalm 89, for instance, became increasingly identified and associated with the life of Jesus. Soon these passages became increasingly understood as referring to Jesus. Through this association these texts, which had never been considered messianic types by Jewish interpreters, came to be understood as "messianic" by the church.

As the Christian year developed, these passages and their attendant associations were incorporated into the readings that accompanied the year. Many are included in the Revised Common Lectionary even today. Gospel passages, such as portions of birth narratives from Luke and Matthew and portions of the passion narratives from all four gospels, for example, are still linked to the passages from Hebrew Scripture that became associated with them. Micah 5:2–5 is still traditional for Advent, Isaiah 9:2–7 for Christmas, Isaiah 53 for Lent and/or Passion Sunday, and Isaiah 25:6–9 for Easter.

The most important issue raised by this ancient hermeneutic, however, is the negative impact it can have on the church's understanding of the Hebrew Scriptures. Liturgically, Hebrew Scripture is often downplayed. It is given only secondary importance and is always subordinate to the gospel. Its role is primarily a supporting one, which either "prophesies" what was later "fulfilled" in Christ or supplies the "imperfect" type that was later perfected by its counterpart in the life of Christ.

Even worse, this ancient hermeneutic inherited by the church year can also negatively impact the church's understanding of the whole Jewish tradition. As Gerard Sloyan has observed, limiting the witness of the Hebrew Scriptures to mere background for the Christian scriptures and emphasizing contrasts between the people of Israel and the church entices congregations to identify too quickly with Jesus, Paul, or the apostles. It encourages us to identify too quickly with those the Bible calls the good and righteous ones. As James Sanders points out, it also keeps congregations from identifying with our "just counterparts, the good religious folk who rejected Christ."[1] This in turn, both argue, gives the unbiblical impression that Judaism is but "mere background" to a Christendom that is the culmination of God's activity in the world and therefore superior.

The second and probably most noticeable way the structure of the year interprets scripture in worship is by encouraging us to focus heavily on history. The church year is unapologetically a yearly rehearsal of the life of Christ. Each year it celebrates again the birth,

---

[1]James A. Sanders, "Canon and Calendar: An Alternative Lectionary Proposal," in Dieter Hessel, *Social Teaching of the Christian Year* (Philadelphia: Geneva, 1983), 263.

life, death, resurrection, and ascension of Christ. This is true even during ordinary time, because of the dominance of the gospel reading.

This historical focus carries with it some important consequences. One is the unique perceptual framework it gives to the community's understanding of the faith. Because the way we arrange time powerfully influences a community's way of thinking, time shapes not only our social environment but our conception of God as well—often without our noticing it.

Take the difference between the liturgical years of the early American Puritans and those of sixteenth- and seventeenth-century Anglicans, for example. The Puritan calendar centered almost exclusively on the sabbath day. Aside from Election Day, there were no other regularly set liturgical days. For the Puritans, the Sabbath was the "queen" of days. It was a foretaste of the eternal realm of God and the heavenly rest promised to all the faithful. By emphasizing the eschatological Sabbath, the Puritan faith became a forward-looking one. Instead of focusing on historical tradition, it focused primarily on the world to come, preferring to view tradition, history, and the things of this world as largely a preparation for the next.

Anglican communions of the time observed the yearly cycle of the church year. Encouraged by festivals celebrating the life of Christ, Anglicans focused on God's great acts in history rather than God's coming eschatological realm. This historical emphasis encouraged a past-centered faith that stressed the liturgical meeting of the present with the past, specifically the past as found in the life, death, and resurrection of Christ. The primary focus of such faith, not surprisingly, was on helping the faithful live the Christian life in this world.[2]

Although the above description is a bit exaggerated for emphasis, the influence of each community's perception of time is clear. Having a different perception of time, each developed a different perspective on the Christian faith. Using a different church year, each came to a different view of what was most important regarding the things of God.

Like their seventeenth-century Anglican counterparts, communions that use the Revised Common Lectionary remain more historical in focus. In fact, even when more eschatological themes are sounded, as in Advent, they are most often sounded within a historical framework, for example, the preaching of John the Baptist, the *Magnificat*

---

[2]I am indebted to Dr. Horton Davies for bringing these differences in the Puritan and Anglican calendars to my attention.

of Mary, and so on. In the same way, far less historical focus is found in those communions that deemphasize the traditional church year. One finds there an emphasis on more eschatological concerns, for example, heaven, hell, personal salvation, and so on.

The historical focus of the year also encourages an overly christocentric reading of the Bible. This raises the same issues we saw earlier in the church year's treatment of the Hebrew Scriptures. By placing those scriptures in a historical framework that is foreign to them, a christocentric church year depreciates the First Testament. It entices congregations not to take the Hebrew Scriptures on their own terms, but instead to read into them a christology that is not present in the text.

Likewise, by emphasizing the life of Christ while ignoring the importance of the Jewish religion of which he was a part, a christocentric church year also encourages a depreciation of Judaism. Such a strong christocentric focus not only entices congregations into a simplistic image of ancient Judaism, it also encourages them to ignore developments in Judaism since the second century.

The most noticeable form of the heavy christological emphasis in the church year is found in the liturgical exaltation of the gospel reading. Such exaltation may be expected of a year that from the beginning was shaped around the events in Christ's life as recorded in the gospels. Thus, it is not surprising to find the gospel reading given special deference. In most lectionary systems, including the Revised Common Lectionary, it is the lesson that "controls" the other readings and determines the liturgical tone of the day. If, for instance, all three lessons are not read, the gospel reading is usually one that is. When other lessons are read, the gospel is usually read last, the liturgical position of honor. In some communions it is often reverenced by the congregation's being asked to stand, or by a liturgical kiss, genuflection, or censing. And in some cases, its reading is reserved only for specially trained liturgical leaders, such as deacons, priests, or other ordained ministers.[3]

However, not only does the church year's christological emphasis on the gospel deliberately allow the gospel reading to overshadow the readings from the Hebrew Scriptures, it allows the gospel reading to overshadow other lections from the Christian scriptures as well, notably the epistle lesson. Because the epistles are often used even in

---

[3]In his article, "The Word in Christian Liturgy," *Liturgy* 2, no. 3 (Summer 1982): 15, Jerome Kodell writes that this reverence for the gospel was in many respects virtually identical to that given to the consecrated host.

congregations that do not always read the first lesson, and because they are often not harmonized with other lessons, the epistle readings are frequently treated with more respect than readings from the Hebrew Scriptures. But even so, the dominance of the gospel lesson can be considerable. Sherman Johnson has said, "The gospels are so important that the epistle lessons may be considered only subsidiary and even neglected in liturgical preaching."[4]

The third way the structure of the year interprets scripture is its heavy dependence on the calendar and structure of the gospel of Luke. This Lucan dependence is not obvious until one considers that Luke is the only gospel that contains the record of all the events that are now celebrated as festivals of the church year. Luke is also the only gospel whose sequence of events exactly matches the sequence of the church year.

Many of the major emphases and themes of the church year are also Lucan. For instance, the church year reflects Luke's interest in historical narrative, which is in sharp contrast to the emphasis on the actions of Jesus in Mark and the theological/spiritual interests of John. The church year has also borrowed Luke's emphasis on social justice and ethics, which contrasts with Matthew's more ecclesiastical concerns.

The most important consequence of such a strong dependence on Luke is what Arland Hultgren has called "synoptic fundamentalism," which he describes as an "overexposure" of the synoptic gospels in the three-year lectionary format. The view of Jesus presented in the lectionary, he argues, is primarily the synoptic one, which for years was assumed to be the best source for proclaiming the deeds and teachings of Jesus. However, Hultgren continues, "We should remind ourselves that the primary use of the synoptic Gospels which the lectionary provides does not necessarily…offer more opportunities for the gospel to be heard…and it brings certain liabilities with its much more positive benefits."[5]

Similarly, according to Robert Smith, even other synoptic gospels are often "forced into a Lucan mold" by the lectionary. This, he

---

[4]Sherman Johnson, *The Year of the Lord's Favor: Preaching the Three-Year Lectionary* (New York: Seabury, 1983), 205.

[5]Arland J. Hultgren, "Hermeneutical Tendencies in the Three-Year Lectionary," in John Reuman, ed., *Studies in Lutheran Hermeneutics* (Philadelphia: Fortress Press, 1979), 147–48.

says, is especially hard on Mark, but Matthew suffers from it as well.[6] To illustrate his point, Smith imagines what the church year would be like had it been based on Mark. A Marcan year, he says, would have no Christmas, no Epiphany, no Ascension Day, and no Pentecost. Instead, he imagines, it would be a year in which we would find ways to commemorate the mighty struggle that the Marcan Jesus has with the powers of evil in the world. Rather than observing the historical events of our present Luke-influenced year, a Marcan church year would concentrate on the Twelve, on the way of the cross, and most of all, on the church's present need "to write in our lives an ending to the gospel more satisfactory than the one provided by the nervous second-century author of Mark 16:9-20."[7]

Smith's illustration is telling, for it reveals vividly just how much the unique viewpoint of even another synoptic gospel like Mark has been muted by the Lucan character of the liturgical year. In fact, even in year B, when Mark is the lectionary's featured gospel, it is still forced into a liturgical and theological structure that is foreign to it, as the additions of Lucan readings during Christmas, Ascension, and Pentecost attest.

Making Informed Choices

Worship leaders and preachers need to approach both the lectionary and the Christian year with a "hermeneutic of suspicion." Both should be used thoughtfully and critically, with full awareness of their power to influence our understanding and interpretation of the scriptures in the context of worship.

A hermeneutic of suspicion means, first of all, a willingness to ask questions, not only about the lections but about the lectionary and the year as well. In what ways are the readings before us intended to reflect the year? What is the lectionary's intent in choosing these particular readings? Why have the readings been chosen for this particular place in the lectionary? How are the readings intended to interact with one another? In what ways are they intended to reflect the Christian year? What is the biblical context of each reading? Are there parts of the biblical passage that are missing from the

---

[6]Robert Smith, "Wounded Lion: Mark 9:1 and Other Missing Pieces," *Currents in Theology and Mission* 11, no. 6 (December 1984): 341.
[7]Ibid., 347.

reading, and, if so, why might that be? What "hidden agendas" might be reflected in the readings and their placement?

A hermeneutic of suspicion also requires a willingness to learn about both the lectionary and the year and a willingness then to apply what we have learned. Worship planners and preachers need to know, for example, about the function of the year and its place in Christian tradition. We need to know what we can reasonably expect of both the year and the lectionary. We need to know what they can and, more importantly, cannot do for us. We need to know their weaknesses as well as their strengths, their limitations as well as their advantages.

Those who observe the year and use the lectionary need to know about the history of the Christian year and lectionary, too, and the way that history has been passed down in the selection of lectionary passages. We need to know about the theology behind the year and the operating principles behind the lectionary so that we might better understand the way those principles are reflected in the chosen lections. We also need to know about the structure of both the year and the lectionary so we can understand the way that structure influences our understanding and interpretation of those chosen lections.

Most important, a hermeneutic of suspicion requires a willingness to occasionally be flexible about the year and depart from the lectionary when the situation warrants it. Worship planners and preachers should not only feel free to lay the lectionary aside on occasion, they should be actively invited to do so. Purposeful, prudent, and pastoral departures from the assigned lections should be encouraged as a means of addressing the lectionary's limitations and biases.

Some of these departures, for example, might serve to supplement the official readings. Important passages that do not presently appear could then occasionally be chosen as the basis of a sermon. This would give congregations the opportunity to hear and reflect on passages they would not ordinarily hear. Such supplementation would also give pastors the chance to strengthen the lectionary's coverage of those areas of the scriptural literature that are now inadequately represented.

Worship planners, for instance, might choose to add readings from the book of Ruth to supplement the two readings that do appear in the lectionary. Worship planners might also choose to do the same with the book of Esther. A preacher, perhaps, might consider a sermon series on the book of Ecclesiastes and his surprisingly modern sense of ennui or even a series on lesser-known stories from the Bible.

Other departures from the lectionary might also serve to address the liturgical dominance of the Christian year and of the gospel lesson that relates to it. Passages that do not fit into the liturgical year, for example, could then be given a new hearing. Passages that by tradition are seldom heard outside their specific setting within the year might also be heard with new ears when freed from the constraints of their usual liturgical context.

Other departures from the assigned lections might serve to highlight the rich diversity of scripture as well. Rather than strictly adhering to the complementarily linked passages listed in the lectionary, passages with divergent, or even contradictory, perspectives could occasionally be chosen together. Passages from widely differing theological viewpoints could then be set alongside each other, letting the juxtaposition give rise to new and possibly unexpected scriptural insight.

Such departures invite creativity. For example, what new insights might arise from reading, at the same time, passages from Paul on justification by faith through grace and passages from James on the dictum that "faith without works is dead"? Or what if we were to read the story of John the Baptist during Lent rather than Advent? The prophecies of Isaiah might also sound different if removed from their usual place in Advent and read, perhaps, during ordinary time. We might get a new perspective on many passages from the Hebrew Scriptures, too, if they were purposely not read with the gospel lesson with which they are usually associated.

The lectionary is too important and too formative for the life of the church to be used exclusively or uncritically. It is too influential to be taken simply at face value, but instead deserves our best and most rigorous thinking. The congregation's understanding, knowledge, and appreciation of the scriptures depend on it.

6

THE ARTS AND THINKING ABOUT CHANGE IN WORSHIP

David M. Greenhaw

This is a time of change in worship. Congregations are experimenting with new forms, and books and articles tout the vices and virtues of so-called contemporary worship. Opportunities to learn new worship styles abound. Nearly every mainline Protestant denomination has a new hymnal, and many have new worship books. This is not the first time of ferment in worship, and it will surely not be the last. Styles and forms of worship change periodically.

Even though change in worship is not uncommon, it is important to assess its merits. Change in itself is neither intrinsically good nor intrinsically bad. It needs to be thought through, however, to determine whether it is fitting and faithful. This essay, written in honor of Dr. Charles Rice, long a careful thinker about worship and the arts, outlines a brief typology for thinking through change in worship. The typology relies on observations about art and its power to form and to transform culture. First, we will take a brief detour through gospel and culture, worship and art.

Gospel and Culture

The gospel enters the world in cultural garb. It must have a language, a body. It is, after all, the Word incarnate, made flesh, entering history. The gospel is never the same thing as the culture in which it enters the world, but it is nonetheless in a culture. The gospel is spoken in a language, encountered by a people, located in a place with a structure and an architecture, and arrayed with textures and colors. The gospel is proclaimed in Ghana with a distinctly Ghanian flair. This is vastly different from Grosse Pointe, Michigan, which in

turn is distinct from across town in downtown Detroit. Human beings are cultural creatures, and if and when the gospel meets us, it is
always through a cultural expression and in a cultural setting.

Culture is a collection of human habits, human ways of being
with each other. Cultures are made up of language and rituals, customs, places, and ways of orienting to places. Cultures include such
things as how we eat, walk, talk, drink, sleep, marry, bury, love, and
learn. We are so embedded in culture that it is as if we were fish
swimming in a sea of culture. As we swim in our cultural sea, we are
often unaware of it. We are so surrounded by our own culture that
we do not even know we are in it.

In fact, it is often only when we encounter another culture that
we become conscious of our own. Many in the West sit down each
day at a table with a fork on the left, a knife and spoon on the right, a
plate in the middle, a glass to the upper right side, and a napkin on
the left side. We remove the napkin from the table and place it in our
laps. This ritual behavior is so much a part of our everyday lives that
we do not even know that it is culturally specific, until the day we sit
at a table with no knives, forks, or spoons, but chopsticks. Then the
previously transparent emblems of our cultural life become visible
to us.

Lack of awareness of our cultural embeddedness is true of our
worship life as well, despite the fact that worship is a richly cultural
event. Worship takes place in a space often reflecting the architecture
of its culture, a gathering of the material structures and textures surrounding it. Stone and marble, wood and steel, bamboo and thatch,
or adobe and brick—each reflecting and shaping its surrounding culture. Worship uses the language of a culture, its rhythms, melodies,
and poetry. When people arrive for a service of worship, they come
in the modes of transportation common to their culture, wearing cloth-
ing appropriate to their culture—suits and ties, dashikis, barongs, sa-
ris, and sarongs. They stand or sit, greet each other with a handshake
or a bow, applaud or laugh, cry out or remain silent—all ways learned
not so much in their worship as in the cultural context in which worship takes place.

As true as it is that encounter with the gospel is not possible
apart from culture, it is equally true that the gospel is not culture. It is
not bound by human culture, and it cannot be bound to a particular
culture. The gospel is multicultural in the sense that it is able to be
proclaimed, celebrated, and encountered in many cultures. One of
the worst forms of contemporary idolatry is to equate the gospel with
one culture or cultural idiom. Faithful Christians exist throughout

the world, and they have received and been transformed by the good news of Jesus Christ in their own culture with their own styles.

Worship and Art

Few places in any culture are as artistically arrayed as worship. The grandest architecture in many communities is found in places of worship. High arches, tall ceilings, smoothly polished surfaces, colors, textures, tapestries, mosaics, and stained glass are prominently displayed in worship spaces. Apart from concert or symphony halls, no place is more adorned with the music of a culture than the worship service. Much Christian worship begins with a musical prelude and a choral introit. It proceeds with congregational hymn singing and is frequently peppered with instrumental solos, choral anthems, and bell ringing. Rarely in contemporary life is poetry read aloud; rarely is poetry not read aloud in a service of Christian worship. The texts of hymns are poems; poetic litanies are read responsively; the psalter, itself poetry, is read; and sermons are frequently filled with metaphor, alliteration, and other poetic constructions. There is dance as well, from a parade of banners and colors in the processional to liturgical movement within the service. Increasingly, printed orders of worship are carefully designed graphically with special fonts, pictures, and photos. The elements of the sacraments are also works of art. The water of baptism is artfully gathered, dramatically displayed, and lavishly poured. The eucharistic bread is baked, twisted, bent, and placed on patens. The wine is poured into chalices from pitchers made of pottery, silver, or brass. Worship is an amazing nexus of artistic expression.

The relation of worship to art reflects the relation between gospel and culture. Worship takes place in and through art, perhaps necessarily and definitely characteristically. In the cultural forms that art creates, adopts, preserves, and develops, the gospel is proclaimed in worshiping Christian communities. Worship is not coextensive with art in all its manifestations, nor with any particular art form, just as the gospel does not equate with culture. Faithful Christian worship selects artistic expression both to utilize the power of the gospel's cultural garb and to avoid the temptation to idolatry.

Two Powers of Art

Art is powerful. It shapes and represents culture; it critiques and extends culture. The taunting song of Miriam, purported to be the oldest piece of literature in the Bible; the drama planned by Hamlet, of which he observed, "The play's the thing wherein I'll catch the conscience of the King"; Picasso's long-banned *Guernica* with its disturbing portrayal of the cruelty of fascism in the Spanish Civil War; each of these and countless other works of art exercise power.

The power of art is twofold. On the one hand, art's power conserves. Art takes the stuff of a culture and orders it. It puts the patterns of nature into textiles and forms them into fashions. It takes the rhythms, melodies, and harmonies common to a culture and fashions them into song and music, takes movements and choreographs dance. It takes images and puts them on paper, canvas, stone, or wood. Art plays with a repertoire of cultural images, symbols, and forms. In this way art is inextricably bound to its culture. It is conservative in that it builds the infrastructure of a culture and plays a significant role in then holding that culture together. Art's power to conserve aspects of a culture is profound.

Art's second type of power is radical. Instead of supporting a culture and its practices, it violates its practices and undermines its assumptions. Art takes what is expected and predictable and does something unexpected. The Guggenheim Museum in Bilbao, Spain, for instance, contorts the expected form of a museum with walls. There are walls, but none are straight. All the walls bend and twist. The ceiling is vast, not as in a cathedral, but more in the style of a cave or a warehouse. A river beside the building is nearly incorporated into its structure, as is a nearby bridge. The usually demarcated difference between a building and its surroundings in this work of art is blurred and uncertain. The building demands attention. It nearly shouts that things do not have to be the way we think. Whether one likes the building or not, its distinctiveness accomplishes a reorientation to what is. This is the radical power of art—to open up to a new way of seeing, thinking, experiencing, and imagining.

The relation between the two powers of art is interdependent and dynamic. In this relation the first power, to form and conserve culture, has priority. The second power, to make culture anew, depends on the first. The continued vigor of the first, however, depends in part on the second.

Although it is possible to consider the first power the less interesting, more mundane power of art, it is foundational. It gives shape to the resources of meaning embedded in the broader culture and is essential to art's strength and effectiveness. Without the first power, there is no second; the second derives its force from the first. The activity of the second also logically requires the first: Cultural critique and change require an extant culture. Unless there is an established culture with predictable forms and norms, there is nothing to violate, twist, confront, or transform.

For the Guggenheim Museum to exercise its surprising variation on a building, there had to first be a well-established culture of architecture and buildings. In cultures of western European descent, buildings have square walls, symmetrical features, and clear borders. These features are part of a long-standing culture of architecture and construction. They derive from and support other cultural elements. For instance, the clear boundaries between buildings and their surroundings derive from a cultural practice of private property and ownership. The architecture reinforces the private ownership. If a building were to extend beyond the bounds of private property, it would violate a cultural norm. By its asymmetrical lines, partly nautical shape, use of glass, and incorporation of a neighboring river and bridge, the Guggenheim Museum questions architectural and cultural conventions.

The same, of course, is true of other forms of art. Painting, photography, drama, literature, fashion—all work to establish and sustain deeply ingrained cultural norms. To marshal the force of the second power of art, they require the raw materials of their traditional forms.

The first power of art requires repetition. For instance, in the realm of fashion, when one sees a man in a pair of blue jeans and a flannel shirt, there is an expectation that the activity is casual, even work oriented, and most likely taking place outdoors. Likewise, if one sees a man in a black tuxedo, there is an expectation of a formal event, a wedding or a party of some sort. These expectations are drawn from repeated experience. The power of the art form, in this case fashion, is in its repetitive use. A black-tie event has very little nuance and mostly repetition (at least in men's attire). We have seen men dressed in these ways over and over again. We know what to expect. Because we know what to expect, it is possible to make a series of associations when we see someone dressed in this fashion. For instance, the United States political figure Lamar Alexander has worn a flannel shirt as a way of associating his political campaign with the less formal, outdoors-oriented, working man and woman. When we see a maître d' in a black tuxedo, we associate formality and elegance with the restaurant.

The second power of art needs nuance and avoids repetition. Because this aspect of art depends on well-established patterns, it needs repetition as a foundation, but it loses its force with repetition.

Artistic forms that were once eye-opening can lose the force of the second power through repetition. What power they retain is only in the first sense, the conserving power of art.

A showing of the French Impressionist painters set off a near riot when their work was first introduced.[1] The newness of this work was so great that it disturbed the way things were. Today, however, nearly every dentist's office in America has a French Impressionist print; they are stenciled on T-shirts and are found on billboards and the sides of buses. The repetition of the form transforms its power. Its power is now more the first power of art than the second. Now Impressionism is more an established part of the culture than a critique or subversion of the culture. It is almost impossible for us to imagine a riot caused by these paintings. They have become the raw material for the second, innovative power of art.

The history of the French Impressionist paintings demonstrates that while the second power of art is derivative, dependent on the first power to provide the raw materials for its activity, the first power also depends on the second for new vigor.

Utilizing the Powers of Art in Worship

Against Change: Utilizing the First Power of Art in Worship

The French lay theologian Jacques Ellul imagines a conversation between a biblical prophet and the prophet's reader/hearer. Ellul says:

> The prophet constantly brings us back to zero. The situation is always a completely new one. Our spiritual life is constantly brought back to the decision of faith, to that corner which our moral, theological and ecclesiastical ruses seek in vain to avoid. The conversation goes like this:

> Yes or no, this time, will you listen to this Word of God?
> But I already heard it yesterday.
> We are now living today.
> It's all the same.
> But you are not the same, you have to decide today.[2]

---

[1]Thomas G. Long discusses this event in "And How Shall They Hear? The Listener in Contemporary Preaching," in *Listening to the Word*, ed. Gail R. O'Day and Thomas G. Long (Nashville: Abingdon Press, 1993), 167.

[2]Jacques Ellul, *The Politics of God and the Politics of Man* (Grand Rapids, Mich.: Wm. B. Eerdmans, 1972), 50–51.

Ellul's description of the need to come again and again to the Word of God, not so much because the Word is different, but because the person of faith and his or her situation is different, holds an important insight for worship. People of faith need to come again and again to the seasons and rituals of worship, not because there is something new in them, but because at each stage and phase in their life they need to encounter again the gospel proclaimed and celebrated. There is, therefore, an appropriate, even necessary, repetitive nature to worship.

Familiarity breeds force when it comes to worship. That a community gathers at the same time, in the same place, with the same rituals of gathering to enact the same gospel, is the way it ought to be. An order of worship rightly repeats itself from gathering to gathering, season to season, year to year. Certain aspects of worship practice limit variation on the basic theme of worship. The presence of a hymnal, which sets a limit on the range of music; the fixity of a canon, which establishes a parameter on the texts of a community; the designation of offices in the church, which determines a range in community leadership: each of these and others are the woof and warp making the tapestry of a worshiping community.

When the community worships, it uses the first power of art to put the artifacts of a culture into the service of the gospel. This first use of art in worship appropriates the culture's images, symbols, and forms to authentically and effectively express the gospel. As it does so, it conserves and enriches the significance of those artifacts.

The first power of art is at work in the rituals of a worshiping community. Take, for instance, the organ prelude common to many North American congregations. The music is frequently drawn from a repertoire of classical or orchestral music. It is played on the organ, an instrument structured with "voices" reflective of a range of instruments common to Western orchestral music. The music signals the beginning of a service of worship. Without announcing itself explicitly, the music encourages a congregation to attend to the events about to transpire. Even if the music is upbeat and bright, its force signals the seriousness of the gathering. Music used for preludes takes on added significance; for the worshiping community it has meaning it did not have previously. Those gathered take the best of a cultural repertoire, use it, and enhance it; they also celebrate it and present it to God. Because the prelude is played in much the same way every week, it "works" to lead the people's praise of God and to help them participate in the proclamation of the gospel in this cultural form. It simply would not work with the same force if it did not have repetition, if it were not essentially the same. Continual change in worship fails to utilize the first power of art to form culture and therefore fails to garb the gospel in ways recognizable to a worshiping community.

For Change: Utilizing the Second Power of Art in Worship

The first power of art is deeply ingrained in Christian worship, and rightly so. The appropriation and incorporation of a particular culture into the worship life of a church is fitting. That a congregation utilizes the art of its culture is fitting. That it uses the first power of art to establish, support, and nurture a cultural life is also fitting. However, if a worshiping community exclusively uses this first power of art, if it only sustains and supports its surrounding culture, it falls into idolatry.

The purpose of Christian worship is not to bless the culture. It is instead to praise the God of Jesus Christ and proclaim Christ's gospel. In order to do this faithfully, it is necessary to utilize the second power of art. In order to differentiate itself from its culture, the worship life of a congregation must use the second power. It needs to critique, undermine, and disturb the culture. It need not do this solely to be capricious, but to be faithful to the gospel that both comes within and transcends the culture. Subverting and reforming the practices of the culture, even established church culture, can differentiate celebration and proclamation of the gospel from celebration and proclamation of the culture.

Examples of the use of the second power of art can be as simple as the introduction of other cultural expressions. For instance, many of the new denominational hymnals have included hymnody from non-Western traditions. Singing a hymn from another culture is one means of using the second power of art to shift the dominant form. It uses the established form of hymn singing, but it accentuates the multicultural nature of the gospel and helps avoid the idolatry of equating the gospel with one culture. Variations in the celebration of the Lord's supper can do the same. A congregation that has practiced pew communion with music in a minor key might come forward for communion, using a common cup and music in a major key. The shift alters the form, although slightly, and enhances its meaning: The eucharist as memorial becomes the eucharist as joyful feast.

These are relatively mild changes in worship practice. Many other changes are possible. What changes are instituted and whether they are instituted should be considered in light of the dynamic the second power of art enables: differentiating the gospel from culture while using authentic and effective cultural forms.

For Change: Utilizing the First Power Anew

Because the gospel is not bound to a particular culture, some current changes in worship are not described accurately as the radical undermining and violating of prior cultural forms, but as efforts to discover and claim cultural idioms more fitting for the worshiping congregation. These congregations replace artistic forms from one cultural repertoire with those selected from a repertoire truer to their cultural heritage.[3] Discovery of practices and symbols more sensitive to the uniqueness of a congregation's cultural life leads to changes in the style of worship.

The largest congregation in the United Church of Christ today, Trinity United Church of Christ, was once a struggling, nearly dead congregation in Chicago, an African American congregation from the Congregational church tradition. The worship, architecture, and art were representative of that culture, mostly of British descent. But those gathered to worship were of African descent, and the cultural expressions did not ring true. With the calling of a pastor, the Reverend Jeremiah Wright, the congregation committed to become "unabashedly Christian and unashamedly Black." The congregation began to discover and recover the cultural emblems and marks of its African heritage. They broadened the musical repertoire to include drums and songs, rhythms and tones more common to Africa or to African American communities. Jazz and gospel music found their way into the worship service. Colorful *kinte* cloths and dashikis replaced the neatly pleated and pressed, dark choir robes. Orderly processions and straight-backed singing changed into swaying dances and rhythmic movement in the pews. Congregational recital of printed responsive readings became spontaneous Amens.

The changes in worship at Trinity United Church of Christ are more a cultural transplant of worship practices than a reform. The worship life of Trinity before the changes was not culturally appropriate to the community and was therefore ineffective. Its forms were from a cultural repertoire that was not of the people gathered or was not fully representative of their cultural experiences. Worship at Trinity changed cultural repertoires.

---

[3]Henry Mitchell addressed a conference of Roman Catholics on the styles of worship fitting for African American Roman Catholics. In Mitchell's address, titled "The Continuity of African Culture," he argued that although persons of African descent living in America are long separated from their African cultural roots, there persist aspects of their former cultural heritage. Moreover, Mitchell argued that this persistent cultural heritage is even more pronounced in the forms of worship. See Henry Mitchell, "The Continuity of African Culture," in *This Far by Faith: American Black Worship and its African Roots* (Washington, D.C.: The Liturgical Conference, 1977), 8–19.

Such change is quite radical, in the sense that a transplant is radical. In the typology just described, however, it is a conservative change. It is the first power of art, selecting and establishing forms, symbols, colors, and styles from a cultural repertoire for worship. It appropriates cultural forms that it can use to worship authentically and effectively within its cultural context; it enhances and enriches them, blesses them, and offers them to God. The gospel being proclaimed at Trinity is in cultural garb, but that of another culture.

Bach to Rock:
Attending to the Dynamic in Contemporary Worship

The dynamic relationship between the two powers of art reflects truths about the interaction of gospel and culture and is important to faithful Christian worship. Art's forming, stabilizing power enables worship to be effective and authentic in its culture; its reforming, changing power prevents that worship from becoming idolatrous. When the church changes its worship, it needs to attend to this dynamic. Inattention to the first power can result in worship ineffective and inauthentic in its cultural context or worship without staying power. Inattention to the second can result in worship that lapses into idolatry.

It may be too early to tell if recent trends in contemporary worship attend to the dynamic faithfully, enhancing authentic and effective worship while confronting idolatry. The contemporary worship movement in North America attempts to create worship services that are more culturally sensitive to persons with little or no church background, the so-called seekers. Some congregations have abandoned classical or traditional worship forms for those more reflective of contemporary culture. The freshness of these styles of worship is often experienced as a clear break with the stultifying styles of a dominant culture.

In fact, what is happening is the use of the second power of art. If the prelude was on an organ in another church, it now resembles the overture of a rock opera, with guitars, keyboards, and drums. Praise choruses with easy-to-remember phrasing replace somber hymns. Often, overhead projectors substitute for hymnals. Bibles translated into colloquial United States English predominate over more standard translations. Casual dress replaces "Sunday-go-to-meeting" clothes. The dominant or prior culture of North American mainline Protestant worship is subverted and given new forms; new ways of imagining are possible.

Like many liturgical renewals throughout the history of the Christian church, this one is based on a desire to translate the gospel into the culture, the vernacular of the people. There are indications that it holds promise of doing so. It risks two dangers, however, if it fails to attend to the dynamics of the two powers of art. At present it enjoys the exuberance of undermining established cultural forms in common with artistic movements utilizing the second power of art. Much of contemporary worship is iconoclastic. Part of what makes it work is the existence of well-established patterns to overturn.

Contemporary worship may fail to attend to the first power of art and overemphasize the second. If it does so, it risks the loss of effectiveness or staying power. The power of new worship forms is partially dependent on the old, the powerful cultural forms that have been selected and enriched in the past and that transmit meaning. Repeated nuance and critique wears thin; it loses force if it does not continue to call on established forms and norms. Congregational worship founded on the second power of art can neglect to use the power in established forms, exhaust itself in novelty, and become little more than a quickly fading fad.

Seeking to sustain the second power of art poses a second danger for the contemporary reforming of Christian worship. Once the second power of art has been exercised, it often reverts; it founds a new culture and becomes the first power of art in the new culture. As such it blesses the culture and runs the risk of idolatry. To be faithful Christian worship, the contemporary worship movement will need to confront idolatry even in its contemporary forms.

Conclusion

Exercise of both of the powers of art is essential for Christian worship to be authentic and effective in its cultural context and to avoid idolatry. Just as art makes worship effective, changes in form and style that make worship more responsive and expressive use the power of art for the gospel. Resistance to change can run the risk of identifying the cultural garb of the gospel with the gospel. However, idolatry can also take the form of identification with novel cultural forms. Overemphasis of novelty or change without employment of powerful, established forms risks less powerful worship as well as idolatry.

The dynamic relationship between the two powers of art reflects truths about the interaction of gospel and culture and is crucial to faithful Christian worship. Art's marshaling, forming, stabilizing power enables worship to be effective and authentic to its culture; its selective, reforming, changing power prevents worship from becoming idolatrous. When the church changes its worship, it needs to attend to the dynamic, so that worship does not lose staying power, as in the passing of a fad or fall into idolatry.

7

MUSIC, PROCLAMATION, AND PRAISE

Rochelle A. Stackhouse

For most of us, there is only the unattended
Moment, the moment in and out of time,
The distraction fit, lost in a shaft of sunlight,
The wild thyme unseen, or the winter lightning
Or the waterfall, or music heard so deeply
That it is not heard at all, but you are the music
While the music lasts. These are only hints and
    guesses,
Hints followed by guesses; and the rest
Is prayer, observance, discipline, thought and action.[1]

T. S. Eliot, in his poem "The Dry Salvages," captures the essence of the embodiment of music and, by extension, worship and the Christian life. Music has the power to touch depths within the human spirit and body that defy explanation, as any pastor who has tried to change the musical tradition of a parish church knows well. Indeed, in the church, music has often been "heard so deeply" that the lived, embodied theology of many Christians comes as much from hymns and service music as from erudite proclamations from the pulpit. Martin Luther, one of the most astute preachers of any age, once observed that music is next in importance to theology:

> I firmly believe, nor am I ashamed to assert, that next to theology no art is equal to music; for it is the only one, except

[1]T. S. Eliot, "The Dry Salvages," in T. S. Eliot, *The Complete Poems and Plays 1909–1950* (New York: Harcourt, Brace & World, 1971), 136. Excerpt from *Four Quartets* copyright 1941 by T. S. Eliot and renewed 1969 by Esme Valerie Eliot, reprinted by permission of Harcourt, Inc.

theology, which is able to give a quiet and happy mind. This is manifestly proved by the fact that the devil, the author of depressing care and distressing disturbances, almost flees from the sound of music as he does from the word of theology. This is the reason why the prophets practiced music more than any art and did not put their theology into geometry, into arithmetic, or into astronomy, but into music, intimately uniting theology and music, telling the truth in psalms and songs.[2]

While Luther does not mention here that preaching can overcome the devil, he is certain of the holy power of music. Can music and preaching, then, unite the power of their differing embodiments of the Word to speak to the church today?

Music and preaching certainly need not be mutually exclusive embodiments of the Word, any more than preaching and the other components of worship are, as the other chapters in this book have noted. In this chapter I raise up several reflections on the relationship of music and preaching. First, I consider how the music and the preaching in a worship service might weave together as a whole to embody and proclaim God's Word. Both preachers and musicians would benefit from paying more attention to making worship a complete tapestry rather than loose threads that form no coherent picture. The enlivening possibilities in the relationship between music and preaching are not exhausted, however, in planning a worship service where music and preaching are thematically connected. Musical theory and practice also, I believe, have something to offer preachers to help them communicate with more power and effectiveness in the oral medium of preaching. Preachers can learn from musicians how to embody the Word more fully. The second half of the chapter focuses on this theme.

Music and Preaching Work Together

In the academic training of most clergy, as well as in the planning of too many worship services, preaching and the rest of a worship service have long been seen as two separate functions. But if, to use Charles Rice's metaphor, preaching is "the embodied word," and music, prayer, and the rest of the liturgy are also embodied proclamation, then Paul's grand imagery of one body working in unison in

---

[2]Martin Luther, *What Luther Says: An Anthology,* ed. Ewald M. Plass, vol. 2 (St. Louis: Concordia Publishing, 1959), 983.

service and praise will become our operative method for designing and implementing a worship service. The parts cannot be seen as separate and unrelated, but, as Rice so pointedly affirms in his book *The Embodied Word*, preaching, music, prayers, and all the other parts of the liturgy are all pieces of one great drama bringing together God and God's people. The body, as Paul writes, has many parts, all of which work as one in the service of God.

If both music and preaching are embodied Words–proclamations of the gospel–then both preachers and musicians need to make sure that the proclamation that comes in all acts of the drama of worship is consistent and mutually supportive. That reality will be enormously liberating, rather than threatening. Musician and preacher are not competing to be the star in a worship service; rather each serves the Word that needs to be proclaimed. Sometimes on Easter, for example, what needs to be heard and experienced most is the embodied sense of resurrection proclaimed as a congregation sings together "Jesus Christ is Risen Today, Alleluia!" The preacher is liberated by not having to carry the weight of bearing that awesome news on her own. Sometimes hymns, anthems, and responses, by their words or their music, can disturb or challenge more deeply than even the best preacher can imagine. Anyone who has ever been to a protest rally will remember how music often moved participants to faithful action with more energy than even the best speaker's words. Part of the message here is that preaching, at least in the European American tradition, is often seen as a solitary task, words written and spoken by one individual. Hymns and anthems draw together more parts of the body to truly move a service into *leitourgia:* the work of the people. The preacher ignores this at his peril.

The most practical implication of these realities is that musicians and preachers in any congregation must pray, plan, communicate, and work closely together for a worship service that embodies one strong message from the Word. It means that preachers must have some knowledge of the musical repertoire of the tradition (something to which most seminaries pay scant attention), and that musicians must have some familiarity with the Bible and the theological tradition in which they are working. It means that both must have an intimate knowledge of what the congregation knows, both biblically and musically, what makes them comfortable, what can disturb them in a holy way, what can inspire and motivate them. We have something to learn from the Jewish model in which the cantor of a congregation is more than an organist/choir director/song leader, but is a primary educator in the congregation who often also acts as a pastoral caregiver. Cantors are understood as intrinsic parts of the ministry team and not simply professional subcontractors with a clearly bracketed responsibility.

What might this look like in a real service? One year Good Shepherd Sunday (in a congregation whose worship follows the lectionary on a regular basis) fell on Mother's Day. The preacher was going to use the juxtaposition of the lectionary and the secular holiday to reflect on images of God and how they change our lives. The musician and preacher in conversation chose two hymns familiar to the congregation using the shepherd theme that would comfort and encourage them. They chose one hymn (Brian Wren's "Bring Many Names") that would stretch into other metaphors for God. For the offertory, the musician chose to play piano variations on RESIGNATION, the tune usually used for Isaac Watts's classic hymn "My Shepherd Will Supply My Need." For the choir anthem, however, she chose the Bobby McFerrin version of the Twenty-third Psalm, which he wrote for his mother and which uses all female pronouns for God. The other liturgical elements continued this interplay between these themes, with the result that the service as whole, rather than just the sermon or just the music, touched and challenged the congregation.

What this kind of integration requires of both preachers and musicians, of course, is advance planning. Clergy and musicians need to communicate regularly about upcoming worship services, especially in churches where a choir sings and needs to rehearse more than one week in advance. It also invites flexibility on the parts of musician, preacher, *and the congregation* as the Spirit moves in unexpected ways. It might require the changing of a hymn after a sermon has actually been written and the bulletin printed. In those traditions where the bulletin in the hands of worshipers determines the service, it is even more important for worship leaders to be open to the Spirit and not to be held captive to the tyranny of a printed bulletin.

The first relationship to be developed between music and preaching, then, involves the structuring, planning, and openness to the Spirit that make the worship service a thematic whole.

Music Theory and Practice Help the Preacher

Of course, it is difficult to portray the impact of such a service as described above, because *experiencing* a service of worship is not the same as telling about it. This reality points to a second important implication of both music and preaching as embodied Word experiences. Both use aural (or instrumental) media. Looking at the pages of music and words in a hymnal or a piece of sheet music, or reading a review of a performance in the newspaper cannot duplicate the experience of hearing, singing, or playing the music. In the same way, reading the manuscript of a sermon or hearing someone tell about it later cannot duplicate the experience of hearing or preaching, because preaching is an embodied event just as musical performance is; you really have to be there, to participate in the event and in the activity of the Spirit in that moment, to get a clear idea of what happens in any given sermon.

I believe that central to the renewal of preaching in the mainline Protestant traditions is a revival of attentiveness to preaching as an aural event. The essential element of proclamation for the people of Israel is the *Shema,* which begins "*Hear,* O Israel."[3] That reminder ought to be posted in every preacher's study. Just as the musician does not know for sure how any written set of notes will work until it is played or sung, so the preacher cannot know how a written sermon will preach until the words are spoken. And just as the musician does not write notes without paying attention to how they will sound, so the preacher should not write without a sense that the words will not be read, but spoken. Not every beautiful phrase of prose will necessarily translate well to the fleeting nature of oral proclamation where the hearers cannot reread the sentence to figure out what it means.

The African American preaching tradition has long lifted up the aural nature of preaching, indeed the *musical* nature of preaching. Jon Michael Spenser, William Turner, Evans Crawford, and other contemporary African American scholars of both music and preaching use the term *homiletical musicality* to describe what happens in the best preaching in this tradition. Crawford defines it as

> the way in which the preacher uses timing, pauses, inflection, pace, and the other musical qualities of speech to engage all that the listener is in the act of proclamation. This musicality represents something much deeper than method. It is an expression of the holy God working through the preacher and the community.[4]

It is, in short, an attempt on the part of the preacher to communicate the Word in the depth and with the power with which this is done regularly by music, to embody the music of the Word.

---

[3]Evans E. Crawford, *The Hum: Call and Response in African American Preaching* (Nashville: Abingdon Press, 1995), 53.
[4]Ibid., 16.

This does not necessarily mean that the preacher will sing the sermon (although there is a long and great tradition of sermons being sung in whole or in part), nor that the preacher needs to be a trained musician. This understanding also does not need to be limited to the African American tradition of preaching (to which I will return later in the chapter), but the lessons involved in this mode of preaching may be transferred to each tradition using the resources available within it. The gift of understanding preaching as homiletical musicality pushes the preacher to incorporate the gifts of music that give power to communicate the Word in the aural event of preaching. These have to do with the way preachers use their bodies, the way they prepare to preach, how they are present in the moment of preaching, and the content of the sermons themselves.

Most preachers could benefit from some time spent in a dance studio, tai chi class, with formal training in singing, or just singing regularly with a choir (regardless of the musical skill level of the individual). All good musicians know that breathing is central to how one makes music, whether that music is made with voice, by blowing air, or by using one's hands or feet. By learning how to control breathing as well as how to use the body to enhance communication, the preacher's written words literally become embodied, the way that music does for a dancer, singer, or instrumentalist.

The most elementary psychology classes teach how body language can either confirm or deny the message that may be given by words spoken. The preacher must pay extra attention to this, for he stands in front of many people who are reading not only what he says, but how he says it. By focusing too often on the intellectual content of sermons and not on how they are communicated, preachers have often had brilliant statements to make that were not heard by the congregation because their voices or bodies were not in sync with the message.

Attention to the body represents part of the attention to preparation that musicians can teach preachers. Most preaching seminars and books spend a great deal of time on how to prepare the content of what will be said. This one element is indeed key to good preaching but is not the whole story by any means. Preparation for the musician involves a continual engagement with the instrument and the music to be played or sung. For the preacher, that means intentional time spent in the source of the Word, the Bible, as well as in dialogue with the Word itself, in prayer, meditation, and devotional reading. Most preachers spend a good amount of time in commentaries, and most could spend more keeping up with the current studies in Bible, theology, and preaching theory. Yet attention to personal and communal prayer and Bible reading and study must also be central.

Those who sing choral music or play in string quartets or jazz combos also know that time spent practicing together in order to tune voices and instruments to one another makes all the difference in the world when it comes to performance. In the same way, the preacher needs to be constantly tuning her voice to the voices and ears of her congregation. Good pastoral care is good preparation for preaching, for only by that time spent listening can the preacher know both what needs to be heard and how best to express it so that it *can* be heard.

Good choirs or jazz bands can also teach us that despite much preparation, what happens in the making of music depends greatly on each person's being present in the moment in which the music is made. Rice refers to this when he writes, "Preaching as a liturgical art demands presence, *being attuned to the moment.*"[5] For many preachers trained in the European American tradition of preaching, this is perhaps the most challenging facet of the traditions of preaching that open themselves more to the unpredictability of the Holy Spirit. This means being attuned to what is happening in the world that day, what is happening in the parish, what is happening in the life of the preacher, what is happening in the liturgy in which the sermon has a place, what the emotional tone of the room feels like at the beginning of the sermon, and, ultimately, where God's Spirit might lead one in either fully implementing or turning away from whatever has been prepared for that day. A preacher who has spent much regular time in preparation will be less threatened by this because there is a deep well at hand both of content and of spiritual openness to embody whatever Word needs to come at that moment.

I once attended a worship service in a small Episcopal church two days after the bishop of the diocese had committed suicide. The congregation entered the sanctuary deeply confused and with great sadness about this event. The sense of fear, anger, sadness, and spiritual confusion was palpable. The service that day included the baptism of an infant, and the child's grandfather was the preacher for the day. The preacher chose to ignore both the bishop's suicide and the child's baptism to preach on a rather obscure story out of the book of Deuteronomy that touched on none of the emotions, the theological

---

[5]Charles Rice, *The Embodied Word,* Fortress Resources for Preaching (Minneapolis: Fortress Press, 1991), 135. Italics mine.

or spiritual questions leaping forth from the congregation that day. He simply chose not to attune himself to the moment, for whatever reason, and he missed a holy opportunity. An instrument that is out of tune with other instruments in the orchestra can turn a brilliant symphony into jarring noise.

Finally, homiletical musicality has implications for the content of sermons themselves. Perhaps first and foremost is that musicality is expressed by how the preacher uses language. Even a tone-deaf preacher learned nursery rhymes as a child and therefore has at least a rudimentary understanding of the power of rhythm in speech. Because most of us read from the Bible in translation, we often forget how much of the language of the Bible uses the rhythms of poetic speech to bring it power, from the psalms, to the words of the prophets, to Jesus in the Sermon on the Mount. Jon Michael Spenser remembers how Martin Luther King, Jr., epitomized the African tradition of using rhythmic language "to communicate the power beyond the literal word. One of King's favorite literary 'licks' consisted of parallel syntax with similar word endings, which resulted in a rhythmic cadence." One example of this occurs in King's sermon "The Drum Major Instinct":

> Yes, if you want to say that I was a drum major,
> say that I was a drum major for justice;
> say that I was a drum major for peace;
> I was a drum major for righteousness.[6]

King and other preachers in his tradition allow themselves a wonderful freedom to play with words the way a good jazz musician plays with a basic melody to give it new life and energy. Indeed, the word we use to explain what happens when music is made is *play,* as in to play an instrument. The preacher is at play in the language, playing the language until the harmony of the gospel, or the dissonance of it, comes through clearly to those listening, including the preacher. The preacher need not be a trained poet to do this, but simply must have a willingness to experiment with his own language and its inherent musicality.

The best way to become good at this kind of play might be to use the resources of the music of the church as a beginning place and training ground. Spenser observes:

---

[6]Jon Michael Spenser, *Protest and Praise: Sacred Music of Black Religion* (Minneapolis: Fortress Press, 1990), 231.

Hymnody, psalmody, traditional spirituals, and gospel songs are important sources of text for the contemporary preacher...Quotations from these sources also evoke a musical state of mind in the listener, not only due to their formulaic musicality, but because familiarity with the lyric prompts recollection of the music; and the listener's consequential responses contribute to the contemporaneous form of preaching.[7]

The preacher has been given an enormous gift in the trend of many newer Protestant hymnals to include a selection of psalms with some sort of sung response. If these are well used by worship planners, congregations will once again become familiar with the powerful language of the psalms, as will preachers. Many preachers of past generations remember hearing that the psalms were inappropriate texts on which to base sermons. This ancient music that has inspired and united faithful communities for more than two millennia most certainly should not be ignored by today's preachers.

The broad resources of hymns, spirituals, and liturgical responses in the whole spectrum of Christian tradition likewise constitute wonderful reflections on every aspect of the life of faith. Just as the preacher works to build familiarity with the Bible, so too, as noted above, the preacher would benefit by building a strong repertoire of hymn texts from which to draw inspiration, theological material, playful language, and most especially, a way into the ears and minds of congregants who may be much more familiar with hymns than with the Bible.

The penchant of most modern hymnals for changing language in familiar hymns (causing some angst in many congregations) actually can assist the preacher in delving more deeply into the gospel. In *Chalice Hymnal*, for example, the chorus to Katherine Lee Bates's "O Beautiful for Spacious Skies" has been changed from "and crown thy good with brotherhood" to "and crown thy good with *servanthood*."[8] If a preacher chooses to address national issues in a sermon, for example, on Independence Day, that word change in a familiar hymn (which would also be sung in the service, perhaps immediately before or after, or during, the sermon) can play into the preacher's composition in creative ways, especially if the preacher is attuned to the varying emotions that might be raised within the

---

[7]Jon Michael Spenser, *Sacred Symphony* (New York: Greenwood Press, 1987), 14.
[8]*Chalice Hymnal* (St. Louis: Chalice Press, 1995), no. 720. Italics mine.

congregation by such a change. While most people might agree that music has the power to unite and inspire a faith community, music has, since ancient times, had the power to disturb and challenge. So has good preaching. How much more effective if they serve both those ends in unison?

Music brings several gifts, then, to the preacher. First, attentiveness to how music (and the other liturgical elements) and sermon may be thematically integrated increases the power of the gospel being communicated in a service of worship. Second, skills and insights common to musicians can assist the preacher in recovering the power of the sermon as an aural event. To claim both these gifts, the preacher first needs to appreciate, study, and rejoice in the varieties and strengths of music that have embodied the Word as long as, or longer than, preachers have.

In book six of C. S. Lewis' Chronicles of Narnia, *The Magician's Nephew*, Lewis picks up on that strength and variety when he imagines the universe's being recreated by God in a slightly different fashion from the original creation. We read Genesis and assume that God *spoke* the universe into being, yet Lewis, very much in line with Eliot's imagery, imagines that God *sang* the world into being, calling the God figure "the first Voice."[9] Literally, in his story, Lewis imagines music as the embodied Word, for as the first Voice sings, all life on earth is created, a different tune for each piece of creation. In worship, the preacher who is attentive to the power and possibilities of music, both as it is planned and performed and as it influences how a sermon is formed and delivered, has the opportunity to join in that creative spirit. It is that Spirit that can create and/or invigorate a community of believers each in search of the Lord's song in their lives and the life of their church. As we attune ourselves to the "music heard so deeply that it is not heard at all," we as preachers "are the music while the music lasts," whether or not we sing a note. Perhaps the greater gift, though, is that we empower those with whom we sing and preach to become themselves the music of God.

---

[9]C. S. Lewis, *The Magician's Nephew* (New York: Macmillan, 1955), 100–102. © C. S. Lewis Pte. Ltd. 1955. Extract reprinted by permission.

8

A SCHOOL OF THE PROPHETS:

Teaching Congregational Members to Preach

Douglas Gwyn

There is a dilemma inherent in the preaching vocation. The preacher is a woman or man of faith possessing (or rather, possessed by) a gift to enunciate God's Word in present circumstances. That gift has been developed through biblical, theological, and homiletical training. It has been exercised through faithful struggle, week by week, to listen and to speak. The preacher experiences a range of emotions—anxiety, conflict, joy, and sorrow—in the process of preparing sermons that edify, reassure, and challenge a congregation in its ongoing struggle of faith.

Possessed of such a powerful gift and in the grip of that weekly drama, the minister who acutely feels the call to preach is strongly compelled to the task. To preach by conviction is to live simultaneously at two levels of consciousness: an outrageous awareness of divine authority and calling to speak in the name of the Lord and an annihilating sense of human inadequacy to do so. I refer not only to generic human sin and incapacity, but especially to my own! This awful prophetic consciousness is best dramatized by Jeremiah, who tried to beg off from his calling (1:6), yet found "something like a burning fire shut up in my bones" when he tried to suppress his vocation (20:9).

At the same time, however, the very nature of the gospel we preach is to empower others. Jesus did not maintain his disciples in a client status. He called them his friends (Jn. 15:15f.) because he was preparing them to preach the gospel, to carry on the work they had seen him perform. He nurtured and authorized them in the prophetic vocation. That principle of extension is essential to the gospel. It is a central paradox that the unique, divine status of Jesus as Christ, Son of God, is established by the fact that he liberated men and women from the bonds of sin, empowered them to do as he had done–or to do even greater things (Jn. 14:12). In a similar manner, Moses asked God to endow the seventy elders with the spirit of prophecy, adding, "Would that all the LORD's people were prophets" (Num. 11:29).

Can the preacher, even a very gifted one, be content to keep the prophet's mantle wrapped tightly around his or her own shoulders? Are there not elders in Israel–and some others as well–who can also prophesy, whose voices can augment and add helpful counterpoint to the voice of the appointed preacher? Does not the role of the lone, professional preacher lock the congregation into the mystified awe of the client?

When a tidy equation of preaching for hire sets in, the relationship between minister and congregation is in danger of becoming sheerly contractual, quid pro quo. That tidy equation is dangerous to both preacher and congregation. It can place a deadly pall over the congregation that expects to receive spiritual enrichment by dint of someone else's labors. Moreover, that passive, consumer mentality in a congregation can give rise to punitive, scapegoating tactics against ministers when "clients" are dissatisfied.

By contrast, a living, covenantal relationship is nurtured by those dynamics in which power and authority extend outward. In one way or another, every minister knows this. We spend much of our time working to "disciple" members into more committed roles of leadership and service in the life of the church. On one level, this is simply a matter of congregational survival; there is so much work to be done. But on another level, we know that no one becomes a vibrant Christian by remaining in the role of religious consumer. Like the moving waters at the pool of Siloam, leadership development is a wave of empowerment that heals those it touches. It must keep moving outward if the church is to continue as an instrument of God's love in the world.

Many would agree that we need to disciple members for teaching Sunday school or leading a stewardship drive. But preaching? Here we enter a realm where the rule of expertise and the franchise of the academy, which are so strong in our society, begin to take over. We rightly value the theological education that adds depth and discipline to our endeavors in preaching. But academic training and denominational certification have strongly mystifying effects. They confer a nearly ontological difference in status upon the individual in the eyes of many congregations (again, such status may qualify one to be either saint or scapegoat).

These mystifications are most dangerous when we as ministers start to believe them ourselves. But if we have learned anything from the Bible, it should include the expectation that the Word of the Lord often comes from unexpected quarters. It may come from a rustic like Amos as easily as from an enfranchised temple prophet like Ezekiel. And certainly there were no seminary degrees hanging from the fishing nets of those Galileans who first gathered around Jesus. The indeterminate extension of spiritual authority throughout a covenant community should be defended most of all by those who know the Bible best.

I have experienced this dilemma acutely as a minister in the pastoral branch of American Quakerism. From the beginnings of the Quaker movement in mid-seventeenth-century England, Friends such as George Fox advanced a searing attack on professional ministry of any kind. Throughout most of our subsequent history, Friends have rejected paid clerical leadership in favor of a ministry shared by all members (traditionally anchored by a core of recognized lay ministers). Today, in the "unprogrammed" tradition of "silent" meetings, many Friends have continued that understanding of every member's share in the ministry (although often with a weakened sense of the leadership roles that particularly gifted individuals may be called to take).

In the late nineteenth century, however, an evangelical revival among Midwestern Friends led to the adoption of paid pastoral leadership. These Friends opted to "release" a local leader for full-time ministry in order to teach and disciple the large influx of new members into the life of the meeting. I grew up in that pastoral stream of Quakerism. Following a call to ministry during college, I went on to seminary and to three pastorates.

I have experienced a chronic role-tension as a Friends pastor, however. My understanding of both traditional Quakerism and the gospel itself has caused me to resist the professional model of ministry in general and the role of enfranchised preacher in particular. The tension has continued despite my considerable passion for preaching. I have been more than willing to preach every week. Yet I have also felt that my functioning in that role tends to disempower the very people that I hope to empower.

Indeed, though my aim in ministry has been to stimulate the spiritual growth and gifts of others, it has often seemed that the better I function as a pastor, the more likely members are to become passive.

That tension played out in a volatile but creative experiment during my two pastorates with the Berkeley (California) Friends Church. The story I narrate here may offer a useful model (as well as some caveats) for other preachers who experience the same role-tension I have known.

My First Pastorate in Berkeley

I completed a Ph.D. in Biblical Studies and Homiletics at Drew University in 1982, working with Charles Rice. That rich experience did not lead to a teaching post, however. I found that many seminary homiletics professors are also expected to teach liturgy. In the extremely low-church tradition of Friends (even the pastoral variety), Quaker views on liturgy can be expressed in very few words, and even those are better left unsaid in mixed company. Thus, I did not find an opportunity to teach preaching at the time I completed my degree. So I returned to pastoral ministry, serving two pastorates in Berkeley (1982–86 and 1991–94). During the first pastorate, I preached on a weekly basis. But we did begin to alter the equation of ministry and worship almost immediately.

First, we revamped the Wednesday evening potluck and Bible study group. I began to use it for group discussion of the text I would preach on the following Sunday. This method was devised intentionally to nurture a core of members and attenders who would have considered the text (and various themes generating from it), would have had some time for further reflection between Wednesday evening and Sunday morning, and would thus be more apt to supplement my message with their own spontaneous vocal ministry. Pastoral Friends meetings typically include an extended period of silent worship— sometimes called "communion after the manner of Friends"– in which anyone moved by the Spirit may rise and speak. Often this silent period comes after the sermon.

We modestly dubbed the Wednesday evening group the "School of Prophets." It quickly proved effective both as an exercise in Bible study and as a stimulant to fuller participation in the Quaker tradition of speaking prophetically out of the silence, "as the Spirit gives utterance." The School of Prophets was a lively engine of growth, deepening Friends' understanding of the Bible and of Quaker spirituality, as well as drawing participants into a more active, Spirit-led role in worship.

Next, we accentuated the more egalitarian dynamic by removing the pulpit. I no longer even stood on the platform, but spoke from the floor at the front, abandoning the use of notes. I continued to prepare sermons in detail, drafting nearly a full manuscript. But after an intensive review early Sunday morning, I left the preparation behind. This method took a toll on eloquence, to be sure. Still, over time, speaking at floor level without a pulpit and without notes worked to demystify preaching and to make imaginable to others the role of bearing a Word from the Lord.

From the inside of the preaching experience, I certainly felt vulnerable without a pulpit or lectern and less articulate without notes. The sermon became a more anxiety-ridden experience for me, as I struggled to remember what I had intended to say next. At the same time, however, I found that the Spirit's influence on my preparation during the week was now augmented by the Spirit's work in the moment. I often noticed that a perfectly good point that I forgot to include might just as easily be replaced by a more crucial one that "came to me" in the act of preaching. Further, the brief pauses that would occur along the way helped the hearers to absorb the sermon.

I can truly say that I was "in the moment" as never before, and I believe that it added a further immediacy to my preaching. Finally, I found that when the sermon was less than perfectly realized, any remaining gaps in communication seemed to act as openings and implicit invitations for spontaneous contributions during the silent worship period. These points should not be taken as a license for careless sermon preparation. I continued to study and plan sermons as assiduously as before, and over time I became more competent at preaching without notes. Nevertheless, I did find that my own limitations sometimes served to empower the vocal ministry of others and the overall edification of our worship experience.

We also expanded the amount of silent worship to create more "space" for the vocal ministry of others. This was accomplished through some simplification of the order of worship. In particular, we dropped the offering and simply placed collection bowls by the doors, mentioning them during the announcement period at the end. (This did not adversely affect the level of financial giving.) We also began to feel more comfortable in breaking the "sixty-minute barrier" when it felt right to continue the silent portion a bit longer. Again, these steps expanded the "space," not only for prayerful reflection but for spontaneous vocal ministry as well.

I left my position at Berkeley in the beginning of 1987 in order to travel in ministry among Friends and to promote a new book. That in turn led to three years of teaching at Pendle Hill, a Quaker study center outside Philadelphia. I returned to the same pastoral position at Berkeley during the summer of 1991.

My Second Pastorate in Berkeley

We continued with the changes made during my first pastorate there. But new circumstances inspired further innovations. The congregation had gone the previous year without a pastor, and various leaders had shared the responsibilities for preaching and leading worship. By the time I arrived, some were weary of the work and relieved to have a pastor take over again. But others had gotten a taste for preaching and for hearing other voices from the congregation. They did not wish to return to "pastor knows best." I found myself returning to an uneasy situation and sought a working solution between these two parties.

During my first weeks back in Berkeley, we constructed a plan. I would utilize my training in homiletics to mentor members who volunteered to give a sermon. Under the care of Ministry and Counsel, our committee of elders, I would convene a group of four or five such volunteers. I would give them some basic readings in homiletics that we would discuss during our first meeting.

During that meeting, I would talk about preaching, emphasizing the uniqueness of the preaching task, in contrast to general public speaking. After a discussion of the nature of preaching and some rudimentary guidelines for sermon preparation, participants would volunteer to preach on specific dates, one of them to speak per month, until all had had their turn. Each month, I would consult with the individual preparing a sermon, providing commentaries and other resources, offering feedback to their ideas and suggestions for appropriate delivery.

The individual would also lead the Wednesday evening School of Prophets, teaching on the biblical text and floating some of the ideas for the sermon the following Sunday. That step seemed useful for many, providing an informal, conversational format that served as a stepping-stone toward the more presentational mode of sermon and worship.

After a participant delivered his or her sermon on Sunday, the group would meet the following Tuesday evening to reflect and give feedback. After five or six months, when each participant had had the opportunity to preach and receive feedback, that group would be dissolved and a new group of four or five would be formed to repeat the process.

The experiment was a strong success. The guidance I was able to provide and the support the participants offered one another generally improved the level of their preaching. The congregation was clearly stimulated to hear the insights of these members and to share in the drama of their discovery. I myself was often impressed and inspired by what I heard. The excitement that each group felt in the process was palpable.

I have to admit that I sometimes missed preaching on those Sundays. I even felt an occasional twinge of jealousy at the enthusiasm that other people's sermons sometimes elicited! But the sense of discovery and rightness in the experiment far outweighed those petty feelings. Besides, participants often commented that their experience had increased their appreciation for the challenges of preaching.

There were healthy discoveries on all sides. There were also some surprises along the way. In my seminary homiletics classes, it seemed that we students were often rather critical of one another. Sometimes it was left to the teacher (Edmund Steimle at Union Theological Seminary in New York) to be more charitable and affirming. By contrast, in these little seminars it was hard to get critical feedback out of any of the participants, so I had to supply most of it myself. I was glad that participants were not competitive, but mutually supportive. Still, I felt it was important to model a style of mentoring that combined enthusiastic affirmation with constructive criticism. Anything less would have been a mere pat on the head.

In my mind, the most consistent and glaring shortcoming of the sermons was delivery. While sermon construction and length were generally good, some participants neutralized their preparation as they mumbled most of the time or did not look up from their notes or manuscript. Although I stressed the importance of spending time to review one's material and of speaking to the congregation, I think that in some cases the individual was simply overawed by standing in front of the congregation. This problem did not seem to distract the congregation, however, which was eager to hear what good news a familiar Friend had to declare, even haltingly. On a once-a-month basis, these shortcomings were easily tolerated.

What was the effect on visitors who happened to come for the first time on one of these experimental Sundays? Did an "amateur" sermon put them off? Generally, I found them to be intrigued by what we were doing and more likely to return because of it.

I must admit, I was not very creative in finding materials on preaching for participants to read. I found a handful of readings and returned to them with each new group. The piece that generated our best discussions was Morris Niedenthal's article, "The Irony of the Gospel."[1] Already a favorite of mine, that article was especially useful

---

[1]The article is in Edmund Steimle, Morris Niedenthal, and Charles Rice, *Preaching the Story* (Philadelphia: Fortress Press, 1980).

for helping identify the singular quality of good preaching and the difference between the gospel and sheer moral exhortation.

It would be misleading, however, to give the impression that these experiments were an unqualified success. While there was general approval for sharing the preaching task, some tensions grew over time. Some long-standing members preferred to hear a sermon from the pastor every week. They were willing to go along with the experiment but grew impatient over time.

That situation was exacerbated by the fact that we also experimented once a month with having no sermon at all. That approach provided a longer time for silent, "unprogrammed" worship, which was a growing edge for some. But it reduced my preaching duties to just two Sundays during most months, which was simply too little for some others (including myself!). In retrospect, I believe that we would have done better without the sermonless worship in the monthly rotation. Over time, it was too disruptive to the equilibrium of the congregation.

A second point of tension concerned the mandate of the experiment. How far did it extend? Some wished to limit participation to the most experienced leaders and members of the congregation. Others, perhaps in the spirit of the Berkeley free-speech tradition, wished eventually to hear a sermon from every member and regular attender. Of course, there were many who had no desire to preach.

Over the course of the experiment, I worked with five or six groups (we generally suspended the preaching seminars over the summer months and during the holiday season). The first few groups were probably stronger overall than the last few, but clearly they were all successes. We had nearly exhausted the number of willing and able participants by the time the last seminar finished. If I had continued in my ministry there, I would have invited participants from the first round of seminars to participate again. That would have brought the experiment into a new phase and would have begun to establish some kind of equilibrium, in which a fairly stable group of members would have rotated in sharing with me the preaching task. In that phase, a more long-term maturation of their gifts would have been exciting to nurture.

The point remains that there will inevitably be a range of opinions within a congregation regarding this kind of participation in the preaching vocation. It raises questions about the role and status of the minister within the congregation. I believe it raises all the right questions. Teaching congregants to preach undermines the larger-than-life profile of the pastoral minister. It reduces the "professional distance" between that individual and the people she or he serves. It distributes power and authority more broadly in the congregation, allowing the church to demonstrate "the wisdom of God in its rich variety" (Eph. 3:10) through a multiplicity of preaching voices. It allows the gospel to be heard through the varying textures of gender, ethnicity, vocation, economic class, and general life experience.

The mystery of the gospel is found in the manner in which Jesus "emptied himself, taking the form of a slave" (Phil. 2:7). As preachers, one way we can participate in that mystery is to divest ourselves of some of that status and pass it on to those around us who respond to the call. On the one hand, we become more human to our fellow church members; on the other hand, we challenge them not to be our clients, but to "work out your own salvation with fear and trembling; for it is God who is at work in you, enabling you both to will and to work for his good pleasure" (Phil. 2:12f.).

I am aware that a number of ministers today are experimenting with sharing the preaching role. There are many ways it may be done, depending on circumstances. The simple process I have recounted here does not require a Ph.D. in homiletics to facilitate. It draws most basically on my own experience in homiletics courses. Ironically, perhaps, I think it is done best by those who enjoy and excel in preaching, those who would be happy to preach every week. I do not advocate it as a way for an insecure or ambivalent preacher to divest responsibility. Sharing the authority requires leadership, a kind of servant-leadership that is possible only in the exercise of a strong gift.

The passion for preaching, like the exercise of any true gift, participates in the passion of our Lord. It comprehends the human passions and gifts that we bring to the task: gifts for speaking, intellectual abilities, the passion to communicate our faith to others, love of the Bible, and so forth. It also purifies these passions and consecrates these gifts as we struggle to devote them to God's glory and not our own ends. At its best, the passion for preaching also embodies our compassion for the people of faith around us. As Fred Craddock has suggested, preaching is less telling people what they need to hear than articulating what they would like to say, their anxieties and struggles, as well as their faith and hope. To preach is first to listen, to the text and to the moving of the Spirit, but also to the congregations we serve.

Finally, as our gifts and ministries mature, the passion for preaching takes us on to the passion of Christ. We absent ourselves in ways that allow the presence of Christ to be experienced through new channels. We make room for the Spirit to work in new ways through different people. Sometimes that happens through the use of guest preachers from outside. At one point or another, a minister also decides that it is time to move on and allow the congregation to find new energies through different leadership. But these modes maintain the congregation within a role as client or audience. Learning from Jesus, we know that his passion includes the time he spent mentoring his disciples to pray, preach, and heal in his name. In so doing, he released an irrepressible power into the world. In following him, we will do the same.

9

WORSHIP AND PREACHING OUTSIDE THE MAJOR SERVICE

Ronald J. Allen

Ministers sometimes lead worship and preach in settings outside the typical Sunday service. The funeral and the wedding are two of the most frequent exercises of the pastoral office beyond Sunday morning. Ministers plan and lead worship for Christian ecumenical groups, such as community services in connection with Black History Month or Good Friday services. Some services bring together diverse religious groups, such as remembrances of the Holocaust in which Jewish and Christian people participate. Muslims and other religious communities sometimes join church and synagogue for Thanksgiving services and similar occasions. On still other days—such as Memorial Day—pastors find themselves in the midst of groups in which religious and nonreligious persons sit side by side. Such occasions are sometimes conceived by civic leaders who do not think in self-conscious theological frames of reference. From time to time, ministers are invited not to preach, but to speak. For example, a clergyperson may be asked to give a talk to a local school group or service club.

This chapter begins with a brief statement of aims that are common to all these occasions for the pastor and the Christian community. We then consider worship and preaching in pastoral offices outside the major service.[1] We turn to occasions that are ecumenical

---

[1]For a detailed approach to preaching on special days within the Christian community, see David J. Schlafer, *What Makes This Day Different? Preaching Grace on Special Occasions* (Boston: Cowley Publications, 1998). While many of the special occasions that Fr. Schlafer discusses take place on Sunday morning, his detailed guidance can be adapted to other services.

or interreligious. We finally take up situations when the pastor is asked to be a part of an occasion whose purpose comes from outside the Christian community and whose connections with the core Christian vision are muted, or even absent.

In order to conserve space, I write this chapter with a focus on the pastor, since the pastor is typically the primary figure in planning and leading worship and in preaching. However, the pastor represents the whole of the Christian community. My remarks about the pastor's callings in these situations can be extended to others who share leadership in the church, and to the congregation itself.

These occasions offer worship planners and preachers an unusual opportunity, in part because an unusual occasion sometimes prompts a community to be more than normally attentive. People sometimes listen more expectantly to a fresh voice than to a familiar one. As a result, an event beyond the major service often gives the minister a chance to help a community consider afresh some dimension of the relationship of the gospel to its situation. At a community Thanksgiving service, for example, a minister might help the interdenominational congregation think about how the sense of thanksgiving in the town, city, and nation could be increased, especially among the poor and marginalized, as the ecumenical Christian community develops specific actions that express solidarity with the oppressed and that express God's love and call for justice for all.

Considerations Common to Worship and Preaching beyond the Major Service

Regardless of the occasion, the pastor and the congregation are called to represent the gospel in word and behavior. I understand the gospel to be the good news, confirmed to the church through Jesus Christ, of the promise of God's love for each and all and the call of God for justice for each and all.[2] The pastor and others in the Christian community are obliged to testify through language and actions to God's love and will for justice for all—whether leading worship at a funeral, at a residence for senior citizens, at a service for the birthday of Martin Luther King, Jr., at an ecumenical Ash Wednesday service, or giving a speech at a civic organization.

---

[2]This understanding of the gospel is developed more fully in Clark M. Williamson and Ronald J. Allen, *A Credible and Timely Word* (St. Louis: Chalice Press, 1991), 71–90; idem, *The Teaching Minister* (Louisville, Ky.: Westminster/John Knox Press, 1991), 65–82; and Clark M. Williamson, *A Guest in the House of Israel: Post-Holocaust Church Theology* (Louisville, Ky.: Westminster/John Knox Press, 1993), 18–25.

However, each occasion has its own characteristics. Preachers can analyze the congregation (or the audience) to determine as much as possible about the listening ethos. By listening ethos, I mean the qualities in the life of a community that shape how people participate in worship or hear a speech.[3] When the preacher is aware of the listening ethos, she or he can plan a service and sermon that are designed to enhance and not frustrate the community's participation in the event. The pastor can frequently make positive use of symbols, memories, values, fears, and hopes that are shared by all, while avoiding striking a match and throwing it on the kerosene-soaked rags of the community's consciousness on certain issues. When such a fire begins to burn, the possibility for meaningful interchange between preacher and people is often destroyed.

When a pastor is getting ready to preach in a setting away from home, he or she may need to collect data from clergy and other people in the community where the service will be held. Such information can also come from newspapers and other media, from local histories, and, as possible, from being in the area and getting a feel for it. When planning the message, the preacher could identify a scripture passage, a Christian doctrine, a Christian practice, or a theological theme that, as the basis for the sermon, can help the community interpret the occasion from the perspective of the gospel.

Here are some basic questions that worship planners and ministers can ask in order to develop a profile of the congregation or group that will participate in the service or event.

- What is the makeup of the community according to age, gender, race, ethnicity, education, class, psychological patterns, politics, religious affiliation, depth of religious commitment, and sexual orientation?
- What are the prevailing values, worldviews, and hopes in the community?
- What are the anxieties and fears of those gathered?
- What is the purpose of the occasion? Does the purpose honor the gospel? If not, do the planners need to help the community reenvision the occasion so that it can mediate the gospel?

---

[3]Writers in speech communication and in the field of preaching have long advised that preachers should know their audience or congregation. Leonora Tubbs Tisdale proposes a practical means whereby pastors can exegete congregations in her *Preaching as Local Theology and Folk Art*, Fortress Resources for Preaching (Minneapolis: Fortress Press, 1997). Her fully developed approach presumes settled congregations; however, aspects of her approach could be adapted to services and settings outside the sanctuary. For a similar way of preparing to preach on special occasions outside the local congregation, see Ronald J. Allen, "The One Shot Preaching Assignment," *Preaching* 7, no. 2 (1991): 41–46.

- What does the congregation or group expect of the service or event? Are these expectations consistent with the gospel?
- Given the relationship of the purpose of the occasion and the predilections of the congregation, what is needed in the content of the worship materials (including the sermon) for the service to be an occasion shaped by the gospel?

When the makeup of the community, its worldview and actions, and the occasion reflect God's love and will for justice for all, the service and the sermon can reinforce these continuities. When the composition of the community, its values and deeds, and purpose of the occasion are discontinuous with the gospel, the liturgy and the message can help the community consider how to realign its understanding of these things so that they reflect the gospel.[4] As noted in the succeeding discussion, specific events generate more specific questions.

Pastoral Offices outside the Major Service

The two primary pastoral offices outside the major service are the marriage ceremony and the funeral. The service of worship at the time of death or marriage, and in connection with other occasions outside the regular service of worship, has the same purpose as all services of worship, namely, to honor God and to help the congregation express and form its relationship with God.

When a Christian pastor is invited to lead such services, the pastor represents the gospel and the church. Through the service and the sermon, the preacher is called to help the congregation name the divine presence and activity in the midst of the situation in the community. In some circumstances, the worship leader can turn to a conventional liturgy. In other circumstances, the preacher and worship planners may develop a liturgy for the occasion.

Funeral customs vary considerably from one community to another. In many European American churches, a funeral service is twenty to thirty minutes, with the homily lasting six to ten minutes. In many African American churches, and in some Hispanic American and Asian American Christian communities, a funeral is often as

---

[4]The primary purpose of worship is to honor God. However, all services of worship have a teaching dimension in that they signal to the community how Christians name the world. The service of worship shapes the worldview and behavior of the community. Worship planners can make aesthetic use of this quality of worship without turning the elements of the liturgy into a series of lessons. See Clark M. Williamson and Ronald J. Allen, *Adventures of the Spirit: A Guide to Worship from the Perspective of Process Theology* (Lanham, Md.: University Press of America, 1997), 69–74.

long as the usual Sunday morning service or longer. The sermon is as long as the usual Sunday morning sermon. Indeed, the service may contain a sermon and a eulogy (the latter being a tribute to the deceased) or even multiple sermons. Many African American churches and others refer to the funeral service as a homegoing, in order to call attention to a joyous dimension of the event: The decedent is leaving this world with its many difficulties and is going home to God.

The fundamental purpose of a funeral service is to honor God for God's faithfulness to the deceased and to the living, to give the congregation a liturgical occasion to express its thoughts and feelings to God, and to help the community receive signs of the divine presence and assurance. As a result, the funeral service should be centered on the gospel with its promise of God's love and presence. The funeral service (including the funeral homily) should not focus on the decedent.

The funeral service and sermon are significant occasions to say plainly what the church believes about our ultimate hope. The church's receptivity to this theme and to other aspects of the time of death will be strengthened if the preacher and congregation give attention the relationship of life, death, and life beyond death in the congregation's week-by-week program of preaching and teaching.

The immediate occasion of death is seldom the time for complex theological analysis of life and death. People are often too tender or raw emotionally to ponder sophisticated answers even to direct existential questions. As a part of a preacher's long-range strategy for helping the congregation come to a mature theological understanding of this death, and other deaths, the preacher needs to plan messages that offer Christian understandings of death and life beyond death as a part of the pastor's regular preaching schedule. For instance, a preacher could articulate the church's conviction about resurrection when 1 Corinthians 15 appears in the Revised Common Lectionary.

At the same time, the funeral is a significant personal event. A particular person has died. The life of a particular community is disrupted. The One who numbers every hair on every head is not honored by a generic funeral, that is, a funeral that could be for any person in any time or place. The pastoral needs of the survivors are not well served by a generic service. Christian ministry through worship and preaching at the funeral should help the congregation interpret the particularity of *this* death through the gospel.

With respect to the deceased person, the funeral homily is designed to help the community interpret the life and death of the decedent from the standpoint of the gospel, and to help the congregation recognize how the life and death of the decedent might help the community experience the gospel. As just mentioned, a minister could select a passage from scripture, an aspect of Christian doctrine or Christian practice, or a motif from theological reflection to serve as a lens through which to consider how the gospel interprets the life and death of the deceased. How was the gospel demonstrated in the life of the person who has now passed away? At what points did the pastor and the community see manifestations of God's unconditional love for the decedent and for the community? Can the preacher point to ways in which the deceased person responded to that love with love for God and for others? Did the decedent respond to the gospel's call for justice? How have such responses enriched the world? How are they instructive to the survivors? Can the survivors complete some of these tasks? Can we manifest some of these qualities in personal and corporate affairs? The preacher and the worship leaders can frequently use stories, sayings, and personal habits from the decedent to give concrete expression to such themes.

As a part of preparing for the funeral service, the minister needs to make a visit with the family to express pastoral care and to talk with the family about the deceased person so that the preacher has a clear idea of the life of the person. The minister should ask the family and friends to identify the specific things they wish for the worship leaders to speak about (or to remain silent about) during the service and the sermon.

An important aspect of corporate pastoral care in the service of worship and the sermon is to assist the congregation in naming its feelings and thoughts (e.g., grief, loss, abandonment, shock, questions, anger). Enervating feelings often come to the surface in connection with suicide, with prolonged deaths marked by terrible suffering, with ghastly accidents and murders, with deaths that take place too soon (especially of the unborn, children, and youth), and with deaths that could have been prevented by a health check or through some other means. The service and the sermon can remind the community that God is with them and can help them offer these feelings to God. The service (especially the prayers) can help the community articulate its pain and sorrow. The minister can indicate that, with the passing of time and with continued reflection in faith, the congregation will again be able to live purposefully. God, after all, is always present. God does all that God can do to help the community create a future in which the congregation can know God's love and justice. That future may be different from the one anticipated before the death, but it is still promising because God is in it. The minister may need to help the church realize that the adjustment may be difficult, and it may take a long time. Indeed, things will never be quite the same again.

Some deaths provoke aching questions. A pastor can help the church articulate such questions and explain that it is difficult to think clearly about them with the earth of the grave still fresh under our feet. The preacher can promise a more thorough discussion of such matters when the earth has hardened a bit under the congregation's feet.

Ministers are frequently called upon to lead funeral services for persons who are not members of the congregation, even persons whom they have never met and who may not be a part of the Christian community. In this situation, the preacher is a representative of the gospel and of the church. The preacher needs to make a special effort to visit the family well in advance of the service in order to be able to speak personally about the decedent. While preachers must handle such cases from the standpoints of their own theologies, the preacher is never called on to pass ultimate judgment on the decedent. That prerogative belongs to God. The preacher's task is to find out as much as possible about the deceased and to help the family and friends recognize God's faithfulness in that life, as well as God's promises to the survivors.

Marriage customs vary from one community to another. In European American congregations, a marriage ceremony is typically twenty to thirty minutes long. Some pastors have not typically included a homily within the marriage service. However, the wedding, like the funeral, calls for the preacher to interpret marriage from the perspective of the gospel. The wedding homily is usually brief— perhaps five to seven minutes. In African American communities the wedding service and attendant customs often take more than an hour and can take much of an afternoon or evening. The wedding sermon can be as long as the Sunday message. In some Hispanic American and Asian American communities, a wedding is often as long as the Sunday service, with the marriage sermon, again, almost as long as the Sunday sermon.

The marriage ceremony is a service of worship. The fundamental purpose of a wedding service is to honor God for God's faithfulness to relationships in the human community, especially the relationships of husbands and wives and others in the familial circle. The covenant of marriage is a particular means through which the gospel is mediated to husband and wife. The marriage service is a liturgical occasion through which the congregation can express and be formed by thoughts and feelings about marriage and relationship to God. The service can help the community receive instruction from God on the qualities of Christian marriage and can help the newly-wed couple and the congregation seek to become communities of the gospel in the household and in the larger world. The wedding service should help the couple recognize how the promise of God's love for each and all and the call of God for justice come to expression in marriage and in the congregation's relationship with the new couple.

The main calling of a sermon in the marriage ceremony is to encourage the church to interpret marriage from the standpoint of the gospel. Given the freedom with which people check in and out of marriage today, the preacher can help the congregation to ask fundamental questions, such as, What does it mean, in the Christian community, to be married? What effect should the gospel—with its promise of God's unconditional love for each person and its call for justice for each person—have on the couple's relationship with one another? on their relationships with their families and friends? on their relationships with the church and with the larger world? A minister will frequently interpret the importance of the gospel's role in a particular marriage by interpreting that relationship through a specific passage of scripture, a Christian doctrine or practice, or a motif from systematic theology. Many congregations will find it refreshing for the pastor to interpret the significance of marriage from a theological source other than 1 Corinthians 13.

The wedding sermon should be more than a collection of helpful hints to the bride and groom. Premarital counseling is the appropriate arena for such advice. The wedding sermon is intended to benefit the church as a community of Christians in various relationships with one another. One such relationship is marriage. Yet a marriage brings together two particular people. As a result, the minister should refract the larger teaching on marriage and relationality through the particularity of the couple who are being joined together. In the process, the pastor can draw on their life stories, their personal traits, their larger worlds (e.g., family, church, vocation), and on how those worlds will be impacted by the marriage, and vice versa.

The preacher may need to pause over particular circumstances that are a part of the marriage. For example, the preacher may need to help the community interpret the gospel's promise and demand in regard to the physical health of the couple or the blending of two (or more) families. Of course, well in advance of the service, the pastor needs to discuss these matters with the couple and with others who might be mentioned, so that they will not be upset when the preacher talks about such things. The liturgy can often contain prayers and other elements that offer such circumstances to God and assure the community of God's constant, empowering presence.

The minister can often render significant pastoral care to the couple and to the church by helping the congregation name difficulties faced by marriage these days. Couples often find it difficult to learn to live with one another. Today's popular notion of romance—based on sentimental feeling and portrayed in glamorous terms in the media—lacks the depth necessary to sustain Christian covenant with one another. The larger social milieu puts tremendous pressure on marriage and offers easy exits from marriage that sometimes thwart God's call for love and justice. At the same time, the preacher can help the community recognize aberrations in the marriage relationship that can lead to exploitation and oppression. In all respects, the pastor can help the congregation recognize God's presence and faithfulness.

The church building is the most natural setting for both the funeral and the wedding. Not only is the church building a home for the Christian community, it also contains the symbols and artifacts necessary for full-bodied Christian worship. For instance, the church building has hymnals for common singing, Bibles for common reading, Christian symbols whose very presence help to interpret the event, and a location and materials for the Lord's supper. These days, however, funerals are often held in funeral chapels. In the case of cremation, services to return the ashes to the earth (or to place the ashes for safekeeping) are often held in places that were important to the deceased. Weddings are sometimes held in a home, on a lawn, or even in a club.

Ecumenical and Interreligious Occasions

The terms *ecumenical* and *interreligious* are sometimes used interchangeably, but sometimes they are used with slightly different nuances. When used synonymously in religious circles, these terms refer to persons or groups from different religious communities. From this perspective, an ecumenical or interreligious gathering could include persons from different Christian denominations (e.g., Baptists, Pentecostals, Roman Catholics) as well as persons from other religious traditions (e.g., Hindu, Taoist).

When used with different nuances, the term *ecumenical* sometimes refers only to a diverse group of Christian bodies. For example, an ecumenical service might include Assemblies of God, Baptists, Christian Methodist Episcopals, Lutherans, and Presbyterians.[5] In this nuanced view, the word *interreligious* refers to the coming together of persons from different religious communities. For example, an interreligious event might involve Christians, Jews, Muslims, and Buddhists.[6]

Ecumenical or interreligious events sometimes include crosscultural dimensions. An ecumenical setting, for example, might involve Christians from middle-class North America, the barrios of a Latin American country, the deserts of Africa, and the islands of the South Pacific. Such a gathering brings together people with different languages, different mores, and different nuances of Christian vision and expectation.

I pause over these matters of nomenclature because, when invited to be a part of ecumenical or interreligious occasions, ministers need to be clear as to what the term means, and who will be present. Worship planners can take one of three basic approaches when preparing for an ecumenical or interreligious service of worship. Each is based on a different theological foundation and draws on different strategies for expressing and forming a community of worship out of members of the diverse religious bodies that come together in the service. Each approach has strengths and weaknesses. Of course, elements of these patterns may be combined with one another.

One approach is for *the pattern of the worship of the host community to provide the liturgical setting.*[7] Persons from other religious communities participate in the service of worship of the church that is leading the worship. For example, a community Ash Wednesday service might

---

[5]Christian ecumenical leaders frequently point out that the Greek word *oikoumene*, from which we derive our word *ecumenical,* refers to the whole inhabited earth. In the broad sense, the Christian ecumenical vision includes not only all persons and religions, but all elements of the cosmos. However, it is seldom employed in this expansive way in everyday affairs among religious communities.

[6]For guides on worship across the human spectrum, see Geoffrey Parrinder, *Worship in the World's Religions* (New York: Association Press, 1961); and Jean Holm and John Bowker, eds., *Worship,* Themes in Religious Studies (New York: Pinter Publishers, 1994). For considerations that relate particularly to Christian communities involved in worldwide ecumenical relationships, see Thomas F. Best and Dagmar Heller, eds., *So We Believe, So We Pray* (Geneva: WCC Publications, 1995); and Thomas F. Best and Dagmar Heller, eds., *Eucharistic Worship in Ecumenical Contexts: The Lima Liturgy—and Beyond* (Geneva: WCC Publications, 1998).

[7]For guidance on appropriate behavior for guests in many different settings of worship, see Arthur J. Magida, ed., *How to Be a Perfect Stranger: A Guide to Etiquette in Other People's Religious Ceremonies* (Woodstock, Vt.: Jewish Light Publishing, 1996).

be held in an Episcopal congregation, following the established liturgy for the day of that church.

This approach presumes that our knowledge of the Transcendent is not generic, but is particular to particular communities. Each community of faith (within Christianity and within other religions) has its own understanding of God that comes to expression in its own language, stories, beliefs, and practices. Our words and actions in the service of worship are a paradigmatic expression of a particular community's understanding of God. Persons within a specific community understand the Divine by entering into the worldview of that community, especially as mediated by its language and worship. Persons from outside the community can understand that group fully—from the inside out—by understanding its world of words, symbols, and practices.

A strict interpretation of this point of view holds that ecumenical or interreligious worship is its most ecumenical or interreligious when persons from different religious bodies worship in the way of a particular community. Those from outside the host body are guests. They respect the integrity of both the host's understanding of God and their own understandings by entering into the worship of the resident group. All are who they are: Episcopalians worshiping as Episcopalians, Presbyterians or Muslims worshiping as guests in an Episcopal service of worship. To be sure, persons from outside the community may not be able to enter fully into aspects of the service without violating their own sense of ultimacy. For example, guests may not be able to recite a creed without compromising their own faith. But the guests honor the worship practices of the host community and implicitly acknowledge the relativity of all religious knowledge by being respectfully present.

The preacher would develop the sermon from the standpoint of preaching within the tradition in which the service is held and from the nature of the occasion.[8] For instance, in a service hosted by an Episcopal congregation, the priest would interpret the occasion from the standpoint of the way in which it is understood in the Episcopal church, taking account, perhaps, of how that understanding compares and contrasts with the understandings of other communities in the congregation. In an Episcopal congregation, the sermon would

---

[8]For comparison and contrast of understandings of preaching in Orthodox, Roman Catholic, Lutheran, Reformed, Anabaptist, Pentecostal, Bible Church, and other traditions, see Ronald J. Allen, *Interpreting the Gospel: An Introduction to Preaching* (St. Louis: Chalice Press, 1998), 24–28.

become the sacrament of the Word, that is, a means of mediating the grace of God to the worshipers.

In such a situation, the sponsoring organization can enrich the participation of those from outside the host community by interpreting the meaning of the service of worship to them. Such teaching might be provided by printed materials or by teaching sessions before and after the event.

This pattern has several strengths. The service of worship should manifest liturgical integrity born from the history and practice of the community sponsoring the service. The members of the ecumenical or interreligious group come to understand the group sponsoring the service by its particularities. This knowledge of particularity contributes to the mutual respect and understanding of the various communities in the ecumenical or interreligious group as they come to understand one another from the inside out. Coming face to face with a community's faith as expressed in its hymns, sacred scriptures, prayers, creeds, and other liturgical practices should deepen the level of dialogue in the interfaith group as individuals and communities gain detailed knowledge of one another. Those outside the host community may become aware of deeper points of comparison and contrast among the religious communities in the ecumenical or interreligious sphere. The questions of those outside the host community may help the hosts reflect more deeply on their own faith and practice: Well, why *do* we believe such a thing?

The most likely difficulty is that some people in the ecumenical or interreligious group may not be able to participate in the service and maintain their integrity. The service may ask them to say or do things that they do not believe.[9] Furthermore, the service may be so strange to some people that they are not able to join its movement into the awareness of the Transcendent. They cannot find the right book, or they get lost as they puzzle over the meaning of a certain phrase. Some people may feel propagandized, especially if they do not understand the character of the occasion.

Another approach is a *liturgical collage.* The service is composed of bits and pieces from the traditions of worship of the various ecumenical or interreligious communities involved. The service includes material that represents each of the traditions involved. An ecumenical service might have clergy and laity in the chancel in their various forms of liturgical dress—some in Geneva gowns, others in cassocks,

---

[9]They may still, however, be able to remain in the service as observers.

albs, or surplices, still others in suits and dresses. The service might include a Moravian hymn, a tambourine and castanets from a Pentecostal service, a litany from the United Church of Christ, a Lutheran assurance of the forgiveness of sin, special music by a Church of God in Christ choir that calls the congregation into participation, a Reformed prayer for illumination, a Rastafarian psalm, silence in the manner of the Friends, a conversational homily as in the Roman Catholic Church. An interreligious service of prayer might be led by leaders of the various groups who each pray in the customs of their traditions.[10]

In the liturgical collage, the sermon (or similar form of discourse) takes its cues from the tradition of the preacher. A rabbi, for instance, would preach in the rabbinical mode. Such a preacher would help interpret the significance of the occasion from the perspective of Judaism, perhaps calling attention to points of interpretation that Judaism shares with the other communions present and points at which it differs.

At its best, a strength of this approach is like that of a collage: each element retains its own distinctiveness, but the relationship of the elements to one another creates an impression that is larger than the sum of the various elements. Each tradition is visibly represented in the service. All persons present can feel included. The members of the congregation become acquainted with some of each other's important beliefs and practices.

However, this approach can easily drift into difficulties. The service may not have integrity. Since the structure of the service and the relationship of the components is not responsible to a particular community, the service can become a mish-mash of pieces strung together in random fashion. Removed from their own liturgical settings, elements of the service that derive from particular traditions may lose some of their meaning and power. Members of the congregation may have trouble switching from one liturgical channel to another: from Lutheran to Baha'i to Missionary Baptist to Unitarian-Universalist to Sufi. The occasion can turn into a liturgical show-and-tell in which the congregation does not really enter into the spirit of worship, but remains at the level of observers of other traditions.

A third approach is for *the ecumenical or interreligious group to create a pattern of worship that is particular to the ecumenical or interreligious body.*

---

[10]For a survey of customs of prayer, see Denis Lardner Carmody and John Tully Carmody, *Prayer in World Religions* (Maryknoll, N.Y.: Orbis Books, 1990).

The service may draw on elements, customs, and patterns from the constituent groups, but the service is more than a potpourri. The communities create a pattern for worship that arises from the common life and vision of the ecumenical or interreligious body. The approach to worship derives its integrity from the integrity of the life of the variegated community in which the worship takes place. The service of worship expresses and forms the core vision of the community in the same way that Orthodox worship shapes and reflects the Orthodox interpretation of God and the world or Pentecostal worship reflects and shapes a Pentecostal view of God and life. This approach presumes, of course, that the ecumenical or interreligious assembly is more than a collection of constituencies, but has a common core.

An ecumenical or interreligious community working with such an approach to worship might be able to develop its own understanding of the nature and purpose of the sermon. The preacher would then be called to preach in that vein. However, I imagine that few such communities reach a level of relationship and reflectivity that will result in their own notions of the character and aim of preaching. Most of the time, preachers are probably best served by preparing the message from the perspective of the nature and purpose of preaching in their own tradition, as refracted through the character of the ecumenical or interreligious setting.

The worship life in the main weekly chapel service at Christian Theological Seminary (where I serve) embodies this approach. This seminary describes itself as an ecumenical seminary related to the Christian Church (Disciples of Christ). Like many institutions of theological education today, the plurality of the faculty and student body comes from one group—in this case, the Christian Church (Disciples of Christ) but many other denominations and theological traditions are included in the seminary community. The basic movement of the chapel service is drawn from the Christian Church (Disciples of Christ) but reflects the influence of the liturgical renewal movement of the last thirty years. For instance, the service typically includes a responsive psalm, which is the norm in only a few congregations of the denomination to which the seminary is primarily related.

Local influence in the service of worship is noticeable in several ways. The language of the liturgy often reflects concerns that are current in the conversation of the seminary community. The worship space includes a baptismal pool (large enough for immersion) designed so that water constantly and quietly flows over the lip of the pool and into a hidden spillway. The movement of the water is an important symbol to the seminary community, and worship leaders frequently refer to it.

The sermon typically takes the character of the theological tradition of the preacher. A National Baptist preacher, for instance, brings a sermon in the National Baptist tradition. A preacher in the Reformed tradition brings a sermon with a teaching quality.

The Christian Theological Seminary community participates in the breaking of the bread each week, as does the Christian Church (Disciples of Christ). The service at the table echoes the simplicity of the typical Disciples service, but the prayers and liturgical actions are broadened to include theological themes that are found in the other Christian traditions. The prayers at the table bespeak motifs that are central in the current ecumenical consensus, as described in chapter 1. In that sense they are much more theologically full than the prayers offered at the breaking of the bread in most Disciples communities. But the prayers at the seminary are cast in the plain but often elegant way of the prayers in most Disciples congregations. These services of worship are ecumenical in participation but are particular to the Christian Theological Seminary community. At its best, this approach results in services of worship that manifest theological and liturgical integrity. Because the service is particular to the community that develops it, it should intersect in important existential ways with the life of the community.

The approach arises most easily from an ecumenical or interreligious group that has a genuine life as a community. When a real sense of relatedness is not present in an ecumenical or interreligious group, it is difficult to create a liturgical life that is particular to that body. Liturgy, of course, can help create a common world among communities of different ecumenical or interreligious commitments that have little shared life. I can imagine situations in which services that are peculiar to local gatherings can become insular, self-serving, idiosyncratic, and out of touch with larger concerns.

In connection with all three approaches I suggest that the preacher openly engage in comparison and contrast of viewpoints among the communities present. Through this the preacher helps ecumenical and interreligious groups to identify core values that they have in common.

One of the most important, if often painful, things we have learned about dialogue is that it is important to name points of difference. The deeper the points of difference, the more important it is that they be named. When we name our differences clearly, we can begin to talk honestly about them. Such discussions are often the points at which we learn the most about what truly is and is not important to our ecumenical and interreligious partners, and about ourselves. If we cover our differences with a gloss of happy speech about how much we have in common, we may create a sense of superficial goodwill that will not stand the test of the later discovery of genuine points of difference.

When the Occasion Comes from outside the Usual Religious Communities

A generation ago, when civil religion was in its heyday, ministers were frequently asked to lead worship and to speak at *affairs that were generated by civic leaders and that were not connected with the historic practices of the church.* For instance, some communities sponsor a baccalaureate service or a service of worship in connection with Independence Day. While these customs are declining in number, they still arise from time to time. Persons from diverse religious communities sit alongside persons who have no religious commitment, but who for civic or other reasons participate in the event. In some places, ministers are invited to offer prayer at the beginning of athletic contests or at the meetings of public bodies (e.g., the city council). Such occasions are often conceived by civic leaders who do not think in detailed theological frames of reference, but who feel an impulse to mark the occasion with a religious acknowledgment.

Some ministers conclude that, in order to maintain their integrity and the integrity of the gospel, they cannot participate in such occasions. They believe that the audience interprets clergy presence on the platform as a divine stamp of approval on the proceedings. They argue that when Christians join in such events, the gospel is compromised and even coopted by the idols of civil religion and worse. Other ministers conclude that these settings, while rife with theological danger, nonetheless provide an opportunity to help a community interpret an aspect of its life from the perspective of the gospel. These clergy hope to take advantage of the opportunity posed by the occasion to help the gathering deepen its understanding of the event and of wider life concerns related to the event.

On these occasions, the service of worship is often planned by a committee that issues the invitation to a minister to bring the sermon. The preacher has little input into the formation of the service itself. If the minister is invited into the preparation of the service itself, then the service can probably take one of three directions roughly parallel to the ones articulated in the previous section. The service could be patterned after the worship of the preacher's particular community; it could be a potpourri of elements that are generated by groups and concerns connected with the event; or it could arise from the life of the community that is sponsoring it.

On civic occasions the Christian preacher has the choice of where to locate the sermon on a spectrum ranging from generic religious and philosophical speech to speaking from the standpoint of one's own tradition. At one end of the spectrum, the preacher seeks to identify concepts and language that will be recognized and received by as many people as possible and will be offensive to as few people as possible. In the starkest move in this direction, the preacher speaks not specifically of the God of Israel, but in more general terms of ultimate reality. The preacher speaks less in terms of God's will for love and justice than of the infinite worth of the human being and the importance of supportive relationships. For instance, at a Memorial Day service commemorating military personnel, especially those who died in combat, a preacher might speak generally on the positive values of self-sacrifice. At its worst, such preaching reduces religious experience to the lowest common denominator shared by a very large number of people in the audience.

At the other end of the spectrum, the preacher might speak out of the very particular Christian community of which the preacher is a part without acknowledging the possibility of other ways of interpreting the occasion. The preacher's message at the Memorial Day service, for instance, could flow from the attitudes characteristic of the preacher's denomination toward the nation and its place in the larger human family, self-sacrifice, and life beyond death. Such an approach sometimes drifts into theological imperialism.

Most preachers will probably seek a theological approach that honors the importance of speaking as a Christian while being in dialogue with the civic arena. A Christian minister representing the church must speak as a Christian. However, in today's world the Christian vision is only one way people in the broad civic community understand the Transcendent. The religions and philosophies by which people live constitute a veritable mall of possibilities. Religious pluralism is now a constituent part of public life.

A minister can offer a Christian interpretation of a civic occasion and bring that understanding into dialogue with other understandings that prevail in the community. The preacher can also help the congregation name points at which gospel values are expressed in the civic life of the community. In what ways do Christians agree with others in the wider world on their understanding of the situation?

Contrariwise, the preacher can point out ways in which the church believes that the civic world drifts from God's love and call for justice. The preacher can explain why the church thinks the broader world is amiss and what can be done so that the world can better conform to God's purposes. On Memorial Day, for instance, a preacher might explore points at which Memorial Day themes compare and contrast with the Christian vision. How does the nation serve God's aims of love and justice? How does the nation frustrate those aims?

In the voice of a thoughtful, observant, sensitive preacher, this approach can make a compelling witness, especially to persons outside any religious community. It honors the diversity of the viewpoints of the persons present. If the tone of the sermon is open and dialogical, it can invite conversation with others in the far-reaching civic world.

In addition, clergypeople are occasionally asked to give a talk to *a group with no self-conscious religious affiliation or purpose.* For instance, a minister may be asked to speak at a political rally or a local social service organization. At these times, a minister is not called upon to bring a sermon, but to provide information or to offer a perspective. In certain circumstances, a clergyperson may not be asked to represent a religious viewpoint at all, but may be called upon because of the minister's extraecclesial interests. For instance, a colleague with a long history of interest in ecology is frequently asked to speak on emerging environmental issues to neighborhood groups. A pastor in Indianapolis who has been involved with labor unions for several years is often interviewed on the radio in connection with local, national, and international developments in labor relations.

At such a time, the minister does not give a sermon, but a talk. However, some pastors are so accustomed to preaching and so unaccustomed to giving speeches that they have difficulty developing a speech that is not a sermon. When invited to a podium in a nonreligious forum, preachers may need to allow more preparation time than they think they will need in case the transition from homiletics to public speaking is more difficult than they anticipate.

At the same time, a minister is always a representative of the gospel and of the church, whether the minister is acting officially in that capacity or not. When giving a few pointers on parent-child communication at a service club pancake breakfast, a minister implicitly represents the gospel and the Christian community. The speech's content and the speaker's demeanor communicate the Christian worldview and its actions to the audience.

Furthermore, in the Christian view everything that happens in life is religious because everything that takes place is of interest to God. While events of the kind we are currently discussing are not Christian in nature, sensitive pastors can often make a quiet witness to God's love and will for justice for all by explaining that these things are the foundation of the speaker's perspective on the subject at hand. My colleague who speaks on ecology often includes a short section in her talks that goes something like this: "I know this is not a church group, and you didn't ask me here to talk about specifically religious matters. But I would like for you to know why I am interested in the life and times of the species we are talking about." She then offers a brief, nontechnical theology of ecology that is a part of her own spirituality and life orientation. The response of the audience has always been very positive.

Of course, when offering a gospel witness in such situations, a preacher must be careful not to engage in propagandizing or to take unfair advantage. When an audience feels manipulated, they tend to discount the message, regardless of its truth.

Preaching (and speaking) in contexts outside Sunday morning offer special opportunities and particular difficulties. The preacher who thinks carefully about such situations can often offer a vital Christian testimony. Indeed, such testimony can have an evangelistic quality as the preacher interprets deep moments of life from the perspective of our deepest convictions about God. Sunday morning after Sunday morning a pastor talks with a relatively stable and established community of Christians or persons who take the initiative to expose themselves to the Christian faith. At an event beyond Sunday morning, a minister may have an opportunity to speak with persons who have no religious consciousness, but who show up at funerals and weddings, at the devotion at a senior citizen facility, or at a parent-teacher organization. Such opportunities deserve our best attention.

10

PREACHING AND CULTURAL CONTEXT:
A Case Study in Preaching in a Korean Context

Koo Yong Na

The service of worship is the immediate context of preaching and the subject of most of the essays in this book. However, preaching also takes place in the context of a larger culture. The gospel message always interacts with the language, values, assumptions, and images of a particular culture. The relationship of the gospel and a congregation is analogous to that of a seed and the soil. The gospel seed must be planted within the soil of a particular culture. The sower must understand both the seed and the soil. The soil makes a contribution to the sprouting and growth of the seed. Just as the preacher must know the congregation in order to plant the seed successfully, so the congregation must be aware of its character as soil in order to be able to receive the seed and to make its best contribution to the growth of the seed.

Race and ethnicity are crucial components in the makeup of a culture. In order for preacher and congregation to be good partners in sowing, receiving, and growing, both preacher and congregation must be aware of the characteristics of race and ethnicity. This matter is especially important in racial/ethnic congregations in the larger North American culture, for these congregations can easily misunderstand the gospel when it is spoken in the assumptions of European American Christianity. In the worst instance, racial/ethnic communities may think that they need to abandon their own cultures and become more European American in order to become Christian. The preacher needs to be able to speak the gospel in the language of the native culture and then to help the congregation relate the gospel and the original culture to the wider cultural context of North America.

In this chapter, I discuss preaching in a particular cultural context by turning to the parables of Jesus as a model for relating the gospel to a particular cultural setting. I call this approach "tensional preaching" because it operates with creative tensions in the relationship between gospel and culture. I use the tensions between the gospel and my own Korean culture as a case study to show how this approach works. I distinguish ways of thinking that are typical for many Koreans from those that are common for many Westerners, and the implications of these distinctions for preaching. I also point out how Korean ways of thinking are themselves tensive, thus creating a soil that is unusually ready for the gospel.

The Gospel in Tension with Culture

The gospel must always be communicated in ways that can be grasped in a particular culture. The preacher must articulate the gospel in language and concepts that people in a cultural setting can understand. This process is sometimes called indigenization. As human beings we live in specific times and places. These times and places are limited. We can hear the word of God when it is spoken in the vocabulary and thought forms that a people can recognize.

From the standpoint of preaching in a Korean congregation, I must be familiar with the spiritual, cultural, and social ethos of the congregation. I must translate the gospel into the terms of that ethos. The listeners, likewise, must make it a point to know who they are as Koreans in order for the gospel to be meaningful to them.

However, no culture is presently all that God wants it to be. Every culture needs to be transformed toward the final consummation of the divine reign. Hence, the gospel exists in tension with the culture. On the one hand, God is already present and active in a culture with the good news, even when that news is not named as the gospel. On the other hand, the culture still needs to be conformed fully to the presence and purposes of God. The gospel calls every culture toward transformation.

In a few paragraphs in the following discussion, I make the claim that aspects of Korean culture help make many Koreans open to the gospel. However, Korean culture is not a perfect embodiment of the reign of God. A Korean preacher needs to help a Korean congregation recognize points at which God wishes to transform its thinking, feelings, and behaviors.

Preaching takes its cues from the tensive relationship between God and culture. On the one hand, preaching should reveal the presence of God already in a culture. Preaching helps a people name how God is present and active through their cultural forms and practices. On the other hand, preaching must help people in a culture recognize that the culture itself is not already the reign (NRSV: *kingdom*). Preaching is a means whereby God seeks to transform church and culture into demonstrations of the divine reign in this world.

The Parables of Jesus as Tensional Expressions

The parables of Jesus provide a model for preaching that embodies the tensions in the relationship between the gospel and culture. The parables are metaphors. Metaphorical speech is inherently tensive. A metaphor is a specific strategy of language. I. A. Richards observes that the highest task to which such language can aspire is to put two things, previously not fully related, together in "a sudden and striking fashion."[1] It always takes two ideas or realities to make a metaphor. The metaphor brings these two components together in a new relationship so that we discover something fresh about one or both. This relationship is marked by tension. The metaphor may name a tension that already exists in the mind and heart of the listener or reader. If the hearer or reader is not aware of such tension, the metaphor may create it.

Two Referential Functions of Metaphor: Describing and Redescribing

There are two referential functions in a metaphor: the function of describing the world as it is portrayed within the text and the function of provoking the listeners to redescribe their own worlds from the standpoint of the description in the text. In the describing function, the metaphor describes how the world appears from the standpoint of the metaphor. Frequently the description is surprising to the hearers because it brings out aspects the listeners had not previously considered. Metaphors are always cast in the language of a particular culture. Listeners from a second culture who hear the metaphor must

---

[1]Quoted in W. Ross Winterwood, *Rhetoric: A Synthesis* (New York: Holt, Reinhart and Winston, 1968), 113.

take care to make sure that they hear the metaphor on its own terms—the terms of the first culture—and do not remake the metaphor in the language, values, and practices of their own culture. This is the task of exegesis, to allow hearers in other cultures to hear the metaphor in its own cultural assumptions.

The second function, redescribing, prompts the listeners to understand their own situation afresh by bringing the unfamiliar or unexpected into dialogue with the familiar and the known. This new meaning is seldom empirical information. Usually it is insight or perspective. Paul Ricoeur rightly claims that the most important quality of metaphor is that it can change our way of looking at our world.[2]

It is important to recognize that when we speak of "tension" we are not simply referring to conflict between two poles at opposite ends of a scale. Rather, we refer to interactions among the elements of the metaphor. These interactions destablize our perception and cause us to think freshly and creatively. For example, Romans 5 and 7 express such tension as they contrast the human being as sinner with the human being as bearing the image of God. The recognition that we are both sinful and made in the image of God helps us understand the tension between why we act as we do (especially when we act against our own best instincts) and why we continue to want to act better than we do. Such recognition of the tensive dimension of humanness becomes a point of contact for the listener to meet the Word of God.[3] From this point of view, tension is not inherently negative. I prefer to think of it as creative possibility in relationship.

Parables of Jesus as Metaphors that Describe and Redescribe

The parables of Jesus are metaphors that are spoken in the culture of first-century Palestine. The task of exegesis is to allow the preacher and the congregation to hear the metaphorical contrast in the parables from the standpoint of first-century Palestinian culture. We do not want simply to read our own twentieth-century cultural perspectives (whether they be European or Korean) into the parables.

The parables of Jesus work by placing two elements side by side and bringing them into surprising relationship. One element is the world as we assume it to be. This view of the world assumes that brokenness, sin, and various manifestations of evil are the normal course. The other element is the dominion of God as already present in the world. This element claims that God is already present in the

---

[2]Paul Ricoeur, "Creativity in Language," *Philosophy Today* 17 (1973): 111.
[3]Fred B. Craddock, *As One without Authority* (Nashville: Abingdon Press, 1979), 61.

world to lead the world toward wholeness, forgiveness, release from evil, and the manifestation of love in all relationships. The vision of the reign of God in our midst places us in tension with the way in which we ordinarily perceive the world. It asks us to reconsider our view of the world and then to live on the basis of the rule of God rather than our previous assumptions.

The describing function of the parable reveals the complexity inherent in human experience and the possibilities that human existence can ultimately unfold for itself. The majority of Jesus' parables reveal complexities in human beings and in social relations in the stories that the listeners do not expect. They operate by getting us to ponder the similar and dissimilar elements of the everyday and the transcendental in the stories.

The parables typically begin by asking us to identify with something familiar and known in the world of the parable. Then the story unfolds to cause us to view the familiar in an unfamiliar way. The narrative creates tension between the familiar and the unfamiliar. By the end of the story, the parable has described the characters, setting, and plot in a fresh way. The tensional structure of the parables proclaims the dominion of God not as a distant entity from the world, but as already at work within the world. Jesus' parables proclaim the eschatological rule of God in the qualitative sense of God's saving event in the everyday. The parables are the metaphorical articulation of the advent of the divine reign in our everyday worlds.

The redescribing function originates from the second reference of the parable, the temporal understanding of human experience. The world of the parable becomes the mediation for viewing the listener's existence from a new perspective. This second reference is attained when the listeners view their own worlds through the description provided by the parable. The redescribing function is to lead us from the known to the unknown, that is, to see the known in a new way. Jesus' parables are these kinds of metaphors, which take ordinary people and ordinary events and from them create the extraordinary.

There are two tensional realities within the parables of Jesus, the conventional way of life as we know it and the way of the reign of God, transcendental, extraordinary, and unfamiliar. These two different realities are each the context for the other's illumination. The parable helps us describe and redescribe our world as the world actually is and as it can be from the viewpoint of the rule of God. These two perspectives are often in tension. When we participate in the parables of Jesus, we experience this tension.

The tensional structure of the parable includes meaning that is rational, cognitive, and discursive as well as subjective, intuitive, and experiential. Wheelwright calls this "tensive language." He describes "such language as tensive because the listeners experience the movement of the tensions of life—stretching and straining, releasing, and relaxing. Throughout participation in tensive language, we are placed in tension with those of the text and stretched or stroked accordingly."[4] Since this tensional language is always in motion, the experience always keeps itself open for new situations.

The Parables of Jesus as Models for Tensional Preaching

The parables are models for tensional preaching in two respects. They point toward the content of the preaching and also suggest a method.

The Content of the Parables Suggests Content for Preaching

With respect to content, tensional preaching hopes to carry out the two functions of description and redescription. It hopes to help the listeners understand the description of the world as it is in the parable. It also hopes to help them redescribe their world from the perspective of the parable. The latter function typically places the congregation in tension with the perspective of the parable as the parable asks the congregation to consider God as present in their world in ways that they had not yet described.

In the descriptive function, the parable invites us to recognize that God was present in the culture assumed in the parable, even when the original hearers did not initially recognize that presence. The divine rule was present in the world in the same way that leaven is present in the loaf—tiny, invisible, but transformative. After a person kneads leaven into bread dough, it can no longer be seen, but it is still present and working. When developing a sermon on such a parable, the preacher needs to help the congregation recognize such tensions. The preacher hopes, then, to lead the congregation to redescribe their culture in the same way. God is present, even though we may not be aware of it. We can now live in the knowledge of that presence. We can think and feel and behave in our culture as if the reign of God is leading us toward the total transformation of every culture.

---

[4]Ronald J. Allen, "Shaping Sermons by the Language of the Text," in *Preaching Biblically*, ed. Don M. Wardlaw (Philadelphia: Westminster Press, 1983), 32.

Parables Suggest a Method for Preaching

With respect to method, the parables seek to do more than communicate information. They seek to evoke an experience in the congregation. Preaching intends to help the listeners hear the truth of the parable and to make their own decisions concerning it. Richard Palmer's perception is vital when he says that we must

> stop asking how art affects us and start with the way of being with the work of art. The way of being of a work of art is disclosure—disclosure of a world, an event in which being comes to stand. The legitimation of art is that it discloses being to our self-understanding so that our own world, the horizon within which we live and move and have our whole existence, is broadened and given greater definition.[5]

Tensional preaching attempts to let the parable disclose a new possibility for redescribing the world for the listeners by letting the listeners enter the world of the parable. The congregation is moved to redescribe its relationship to its culture from the perspective of the parable.

In the tension between the world of the parable and the world of the listener, tensionality leads the hearer into visionary insights in which the hearer experiences God's present rule. In the process, tensional preaching hopes that the congregation makes the transition from information about faith to the experience of faith. It helps communicate even the nonrational in human experience and appeals not only to the thinker inside of us, but to the artist as well, for "faith itself requires an imaginative leap."[6]

The tensional sermon works like the parable. The sermon does not typically begin with a confrontation. The sermon asks us to identify with something familiar in our world. Then the sermon unfolds to cause us to view the familiar in an unfamiliar way. The sermon creates tension between the familiar and the unfamiliar, between the world of our conventional assumptions and the world as it can be from the perspective of the reign of God. By the end of the sermon, the preacher has described an aspect of our world from the point of view of the fresh awareness of God's dominion. The listeners recognize

---

[5]Richard E. Palmer, *Hermeneutics* (Evanston, Ill.: Northwestern University Press, 1969), 241.

[6]Janice Riggle Huie, "Preaching Through Metaphor," in *Women Ministers: How Women Are Redefining Traditional Roles*, ed. Judith L. Weidman (San Francisco: Harper and Row, 1981), 56.

God not as an entity distant from our setting, but as already at work among us. We must decide, then, how we respond to this divine presence.

Leading Motifs in Korean Culture

I now turn to Korean culture as a case study in how tensional sermons can help a preacher relate the gospel to a particular cultural context. I will illuminate ways of thinking that are common to many Koreans, and along the way I will comment on how that way of thinking differs from patterns of thinking that are often found in the West.

I begin with this general observation: Whereas many people in other societies tackle issues individually and in a linear manner, Korean people (like many other Asian peoples) tend to consider each of the issue's components and their relationships with one another. This relational perspective in almost every stance of life is at the heart of what is known as "Koreanness." There are two types of Korean ethos, essential and existential.[7]

The Essential Ethos: *Hahn, Jung,* and *Mut*

The essential ethos is *hahn, jung,* and *mut.*[8] We can find here the essential ethos of different religions and philosophies that have existed in Korea in the past and that still operate in much Korean thinking and behavior today.

Hahn: *The Essence of the Mind for Many Koreans*

Hahn is the major mode, or essence, of the mind for many Koreans.[9] *Hahn* is a purely Korean word and can be translated into many different words with many different nuances of meaning. Basically, *hahn* means "the great," "the absolute." It denotes divine supremacy. It designates the Supreme Being, *hahn-nim* or *hahn-u-nim.* The word *hahn-nim* is a compound word. The first word means "heaven" and the second, "the honorable one." *Hahn* is a root to be used in Korean words like *hahn-Kook* (Korea), *hahn-Kyo-re* (Korean people), *hahn-Keul* (Korean language), and *hahn-Url* (Korean soul). The word *hahn* is used to express Korean identity.

Second, *hahn* means "Oneness." It is one and the totality at the same time. *Hahn* bases its philosophical model on a circle. Seeing the

---

[7]Andrew Sung Park, *Racial Conflict and Healing: An Asian-American Theological Perspective* (Maryknoll, N.Y.: Orbis Books, 1996), 107.

[8]Ibid.

[9]Sang Yil Kim, *Hahn* (Seoul, Korea: Onnuri, 1986), 7.

beginning and the end within the scope of one glance, it refuses to isolate any one of the ends, but instead links them together in a single circle.[10] The *hahn* mind sees both the forest and its trees, the ocean and its water simultaneously.

The principle of "Oneness" shows its inclusiveness in two of the following ideas: "one-in-many" and "many-in-one." Its inclusive character embraces even the opposite extremes. The holy and the secular belong to each other. While the two terms exist in their own particularities, they still meet each other without contradiction. *Hahn* symbolizes paradoxical inclusiveness.[11]

> In *hahn,* the part unrolls the whole and the whole "envelopes" the part. *Hahn* can mean the whole and the part without self-contradiction; in the same notion of *hahn,* the two terms coexist naturally. The Beauty of *hahn* is that ontological antithesis (whole and part) are united in paradoxical harmony (oneness). The *hahn* mind embraces Yin and Yang, "either...or" and "both...and" without self-contradiction.[12]

The Korean understanding of God and salvation begins at this point. In some other systems of belief, the Transcendent Being is an untouchable, reigning from a place far above the world. However, Korean thought tends to suggest that God is seen and found in every substance within the world, whether in nature or person. We can experience the God who already lives in culture. *Hahn* contains such an inclusive harmony.

This relationship between "one" and "many" has been the problematic issue for Buddhism, Confucianism, and several streams of Western philosophy. The question of the relationship between universal and particular, transcendence and immanence, and God and world has always been the problematic issue of "one-and-many." Several leading Western philosophers have tried to solve this issue with the idea of "both/and" or "either/or." Several strands of Asian thought have tried to solve the issue in the idea of "neither/nor." It means that "one-and-many" are the same. It also means that there is no "one-or-many" but only the "middle." It negates "one-and-many" and takes the "middle" or "about." Korean Buddhism and Confucianism went beyond the concept of the "middle" to that of "about."

A dominant perspective in the Korean mind tries to solve the issue of "one-and-many" in relationality. We find it in the concept of

---

[10]Ibid., 108.
[11]Ibid.
[12]Ibid.

tensionality. The tensional relationship that exists between "one" and "many" is always in motion. Although these two terms exist independently, they are never static. They exist and ultimately function in coherence with one another to create the resultant product, that is, meaning.

In developing the theory of tensionality, we find Yulgok's thought extremely helpful. Yulgok (1536–1584), a prominent Korean Confucian scholar, used neo-Confucianism as a medium for expressing the *hahn* mind.[13] The fundamental conceptual components of the thought system of neo-Confucian cosmology and ontology are *taegeuk, yin, yang, li, ki,* and the interrelationship of these ideas.[14]

Taegeuk is the focal point of the neo-Confucian cosmology and ontology. It became the symbol for both the innerworld (self) and the outerworld (cosmos). It represents the relationship of humanity and the cosmos.[15] The literal meaning of the word *taegeuk* is the combination of two Chinese words, *tae* (great, supreme) and *geuk* (ultimate). The English translation, the great ultimate, should not suggest that the fundamental nature of *taegeuk* is the "final (ultimate) entity," although it has a sense of "finality," or "irreducibility."[16]

Taegeuk is not an entity. It always includes within itself two polarities or two opposite aspects. These polarities, nevertheless, are neither separable nor identical. They cannot be separated, but should be distinguished. The fundamental nature of the two polarities of *taegeuk* is not lost, nor do the polarities contradict one another. They distinguish themselves from each other yet correspond to each other.

When we look into the structure of *taegeuk,* we see the subtle movement of the alteration of *yin* (shadow) and *yang* (brightness).[17] These concepts of *yin* and *yang* cannot be understood in isolation, but always in relationship to one another. Moreover, they are intrinsically dependent on each other for their constitutive elements. They are related to each other in an organic way.

The inclusiveness in *yin* and *yang* is an important character for our hermeneutic theory of preaching. *Yin* includes *yang* and conversely

---

[13]Ibid., 109.

[14]Young Chan Ro, "Yulgok's Idea of Taegeuk and its Implication for the Korean Way of Thinking," in *Essays on Korean Heritage and Christianity,* ed. Sang Hyun Lee (Princeton, N.J.: Princeton University Press, 1984), 170.

[15]Ibid., 172.

[16]Ibid.

[17]Ibid., 175.

yang includes *yin*.[18] *Yin* and *yang* are relational. One cannot exist without the other. Likewise, God cannot be understood without the human being, and the human being cannot exist without God. The inner, connecting principle cannot exist by itself. It always exists in the relationship.

There is also a complementary characteristic in the *yin* and *yang* relationship that can be explained with the conjunction "and." Because of this "and," *yin* cannot exist without *yang*, nor *yang* without *yin*. This codependence is due to the "and," the connecting principle.[19] The organizing principle "and" has the characteristics of "both/and" and of "between." The principle "between" then suggests that with the existing two comes an inclination for a third party as well.

This network of notions is a significant point of contact between Koreanness, the gospel, and the parables of Jesus. The preacher can point out that the parables, like this common Korean perspective, assume that the Divine is already present and at work in culture. While *hahn* is not the equivalent of the rule of God, the concept of *hahn* prepares the Korean congregation to understand the rule of God. For *hahn* points toward the ultimate harmony or oneness in relationship that is the hallmark of the divine rule in the Jewish and Christian traditions.

Jung: *The Affection and Compassionate Attachment of Each for the Other*

Jung is an affectionate attachment. Koreans use this word to express warm feelings. Many compound words are made with *jung* for such feelings. They are "the consolidation of emotion (*jung-suh*), affection (*ae-jung*), passion (*yul-jung*), sentiment (*jung-cho*), human-heartedness (*ihn-jung*), sympathy (*dong-jung*), and heart (*shim-jung*)."[20] Jung is the feeling of endearment (*jung-dah-um*). The ethos of the Korean heart is *jung-ful*. *Jung* is the warmth of such human-heartedness. It overwhelms the business mind. Koreans communicate from heart to heart with their mutual care and *jung*. *Jung* is compassionate attachment.[21]

[18]Jung Young Lee, *The Trinity in Asian Perspective* (Nashville: Abingdon Press, 1996), 58.
[19]Ibid., 59.
[20]Park, *Racial Conflict and Healing*, 110.
[21]Ibid., 111.

Because Koreans have suffered throughout history, they are filled with *jung* when they see others suffering. The feeling of *jung* arises compassionately when people share their deep hurts. *Jung* strengthens the bonding of the relationship between two persons.

The concept of *jung* for many Koreans can be distinguished from that of love for many Westerners. *Jung* is more indirect in emotional expression, more affective, more relational, more inward, more naturally developing, more unconditional, more fused, and less differentiated. The concept of love in the Western mind is a more direct expression, more physical and behavioral, more action-oriented, more need/desire-related, more intentional, more contractual, more possessive, and more differentiated with boundary.[22] *Jung* represents a symbolic world of being more fused and less separated in the individual/separation process. It has the quality of interdependency.[23]

Jung is also a signficant point of correspondence between Koreanness, the gospel, and the parables of Jesus. Jung describes an essential quality of community: the mutual relationship of all members. This is one of the most important motifs in the reign of God. It is in tension, of course, with the individualistic urge that is typical of many European Americans. This tendency toward individualism is even appearing among some Korean Americans. The motif of *jung*, as enhanced by the gospel, can be a powerful antidote to individualism.

Mut: *The Ultimate Beauty of Life*

Mut is the other important Korean ethos. It may be translated as "beauty of natural harmony," "splendor of asymmetry," or "grace of gentleness."[24] Sung Bum Yun (1916–1980) and Dong Shik Ryu (born 1922) underscore this aspect of Koreanness. Yun explains the Korean spirituality in three concepts: *gam,* which is the content of the gospel; *somssi,* the cultural a priori; and *mut,* the ultimate beauty of life. The ultimate beauty of life (*mut*) occurs when the gospel meets the culture for the person.[25]

Ryu expresses Korean spirituality in three concepts: *Hahn* (the transcendental divine), *mut* (ultimate beauty of completeness), and *sam* (existential living). *Mut* is created in the harmonious meeting of

---

[22]Luke I. Kim, "Korean Ethos," in *Proceedings of the Winter Conference of the American Academy of Psychoanalysis* (San Antonio, Tex., December 8, 1990), 13.

[23]Ibid., 16.

[24]Park, *Racial Conflict and Healing,* 112.

[25]Sung Bum Yun, *Korean Religious Culture and Korean Christianity* (Seoul: Seoul Methodist Seminary Press, 1998), 17–39.

hahn (the Divine) and life (human reality).[26] Although Yun and Ryu use different concepts to explain Korean spirituality, they both understand *mut* as something that occurs in the meeting of the gospel and the culture. "The incarnation of hahn in jung produces the elegance of mut. When we embody the idea of hahn in the life of jung, mut flows from it."[27] The goal of life for Koreans is to live in *mut. Mut,* as just described, is a quality inherent in the reign of God.

The Existential Ethos

The existential ethos is *han,* the ineffable agony of the *Minjung* (oppressed people). We can find the existential ethos in the social and political world.

Han: *Suppressed Anger*

Han is the opposite of *jung. Han* refers to suppressed anger, hate, despair, the holding of a grudge, or feelings of everlasting woe.[28] It is not simply a private emotion, but a pervasively collective and emotional state among Koreans, who have historically experienced tragedies and pain in their lives. Koreans struggled through wars, political and social upheavals, the caste system, and oppression of the poor and powerless.

As a result, Koreans have accumulated deep feelings of *han:* suppressed anger, resentment, and underlying depression.[29] *Han* is a frustrated hope, a collapsed feeling of pain rooted in the anguish of a victim. Unresolved resentment against injustice epitomizes the state of *han,* which is expressed through feelings of abandonment and helplessness. *Han* is the victimization syndrome. Buddhism tends to ignore *han,* while Confucian tradition suppresses *han* through self-discipline. Contrary to these "high-minded" religions, shamanism releases *han* in a process called *han-puri* (unknot).[30]

Since shamanism, as a Korean folk belief, releases people from the negative effects of *han,* we need to discuss it. The shaman (*mudang* in Korean) is a recognized professional who interprets the words and visions of gods. Korean shamanism is a people's folk faith that releases their *han* (victimization syndrome). A *mudang* understands a

---

[26]Dong Shik Ryn, *Poong Ryun Do and Korean Religious Thought* (Seoul: Yun Se University Press, 1997), 68.

[27]Park, *Racial Conflict and Healing,* 113.

[28]Kim, "Korean Ethos," 17.

[29]Ibid., 18.

[30]David Kwang-sun Suh, "Korean Shamanism: The Religion of Han," in *Essays on Korean Heritage and Christianity,* 50–56.

person's grievances and sufferings and, through a shamanistic ritual, resolves the person's *han*. Because Korean Christianity finds its deepest roots in shamanism, it inevitably tapers down and finds a connection as well in the minds of the *minjung* (the oppressed people) of Korea. As a result of this connection, Christianity in Korea grows in numbers, becoming one of the most powerful and dynamic religions in Korea today. Thus, we see that the nature of "Korean Christianity, although so western in its liturgy and appearance, is obviously quite shamanistic in its belief and behavior."[31]

The reign of God, of course, intends to end all distortions of life in the world. This reign promises the Korean people that God is at work in the world to end the repressions of life that are associated with *han*. This news is welcome to many Koreans, who have been oppressed in many ways (e.g., by other nations, by economic deprivation, by social inequity) for many, many centuries.

To summmarize, the phenomenon of Koreanness can be explained in the concepts of *hahn, jung, mut,* and *han* and the relationship among them. Indeed, relationality is the key for much Korean thinking in regard to understanding the Divine, the human'situation, and the ultimate goal of human life.

Tensional Preaching in a Korean Context

Structurally, Koreanness is much like a metaphor. A metaphor deals with two elements and their relationships with each other. Likewise, Koreanness does the same. Within the framework of Koreanness lie elements of *yin* and *yang,* the transcendental and the everyday, one and many, and so forth. The metaphorical structure of Koreanness provides a natural soil for the preacher to develop a tensional sermon.

The Inclusivity of the Hahn *Mind*

The *hahn* mind is inclusive. In the transcendental *hahn* there is already an immanence of everyday living. This idea of inclusiveness affirms the culture, for God is already present in each culture, ethnicity, and race. We can take Adam and Eve as an example. The first persons created, they were purposed to be human beings in God's image. They were the prototypes of all human beings. So our essence as human beings, within specific cultures, is divinely God-purposed. God meets us in the depths of our being. As Paul understood in Acts 17:22–28, God is, at the same time, a transcendental being and the foundation

---

of our being. We are then called, within our specificities, to follow in that image of God. Therefore, a purpose of gospel preaching in a Korean context is to help Koreans recognize that we are made in the image of God.[32]

The *hahn* mind respects every person because each person is a house of the Divine. In this sense redemption does not precede or replace the creation-purpose of their Koreanness.[33] The *hahn* mind sees ethnic/racial differences as great assets. This characteristic of inclusiveness is not judgmental toward other ethnic/racial congregations. This inclusiveness signifies the revealing function of God, who is already in the everyday. These revealing functions complement each other.

The Process of Change

The mind of the Korean, as expressed in Yulgok's thought, sees reality in the very process of change. Reality is process. This implies that reality cannot be separated from the two primordial forces (*yin* and *yang*) of the universe, but is found rather in the process of an interaction between them.[34] This idea of change signifies the nature of preaching as an event. Preaching should be an event that happens in the relationship between the gospel and the listener.

Openness of Life

The Korean mind highlights openness of life. It accepts the ambivalent reality of one-in-many and many-in-one. It supports a multiplex mode of thinking. A sermon may be structured in tension to be open-ended. Preaching needs to be open-ended because the listener must actively participate in hearing the gospel.

Relationality in Tension

The Korean mind recognizes the part (one) and the whole (many) simultaneously. These two terms coexist naturally without self-contradiction. Their existence becomes meaningful only in their tensional relationship to each other. The word "tension" does not carry with it a negative connotation. It leans instead toward a more creative relationality. The two different terms never stand still but are always in motion in order to produce a third element. The characteristic of this third element is created in the relation to the

[32]Ibid., 114–15.
[33]Ibid., 115.
[34]Ro, "Yulgok's Idea of Taegeuk," 179.

tensional relationship of the part and the whole. This third element is "meaning." Preaching exists for this third element that occurs only when the gospel and the congregation are present.

The Transforming Character of Tensionality

There is tension between *jung* (affectionate attachment) and *han* (suppressed anger). *Han,* being the opposite of *jung,* needs to be resolved or overcome by *jung.* In this sense, one term (*han*) is transformed by the other (*jung*). When this transformation has occurred, *mut* (ultimate, artful completeness of life) is the result. This character of transformation, different from that of inclusiveness, must be recognized as the character of preaching. Preaching must have a complementary function to the reality of life as well as a transforming function. While preaching should reveal the presence of God already in culture, it must transform the culture toward a final consummation of the reign of God. A sermon may be structured in tension in order to have the complementing and transforming functions at the same time.

The gospel is the power of God for salvation to everyone (Rom. 1:16). A priori, the gospel is present for every ethnic/racial group. From the beginning, God has communicated with human beings. However, in order for people to appreciate the gospel fully, it must come to people in language and concepts that they can understand. The gospel is most fully received and expressed only through everyone's own culture. At the same time, people must realize that the gospel transcends every formulation of it. Indeed, as Andrew Park notices, there is no single Christian culture.[35] There is no culture that is completely Christian. There are diverse cultures, each of which has points that are particularly promising as contacts with the gospel and points that frustrate the gospel. All cultures need to be transformed toward the reign of God.

The Korean mind and the parables of Jesus can contribute to a fresh paradigm of preaching for the multicultural world of today. People in many cultures live in religious pluralism and social uncertainty. Human beings struggle between who we are and what we ought to be. The concepts of "either/or" or "both/and" seldom give satisfactory answers to such struggles. The Korean notion of *hahn,* and its attendant motifs, offers many preachers a way of handling differences that does not degenerate into exclusive dualisms. *Hahn*

---

[35]Park, *Racial Conflict and Healing,* 103.

allows a people to live with several perspectives simultaneously, recognizing the value in each, and recognizing ways in which the many are related as one. While *hahn* is not the equivalent of the reign of God, *hahn* thinking moves many people in that direction.

For its part, tensional preaching may provide us with a way of helping congregations encounter the gospel afresh. It can help people in the congregation recognize tensions between the rule of God and our present broken ways of thinking, feeling, and behaving. Having lived in North America a long time, I have come to think that such preaching may help European Americans recognize the limitations in their tendencies to think in exclusive categories (either/or) and to move toward understanding the relativities of such categories in the reign of God.

When these things happen, preaching becomes an event. The inclusiveness, the openness, the eventfulness of the tensional preaching contributes to ways that the gospel is heard in congregations of many ethnicities and races.